Dom Helder Camara
THE CONVERSIONS
OF A BISHOP

Dom Helder Camara

THE CONVERSIONS
OF A BISHOP

an interview with
José de Broucker

Translated by Hilary Davies

COLLINS

Published by Collins
London · Glasgow · Cleveland · New York
Toronto · Sydney · Auckland · Johannesburg

First published as *Dom Helder Camara:*
Les Conversions d'un Évêque by Éditions
du Seuil, Paris.

© Éditions du Seuil, 1977

First published in Great Britain 1979
UK ISBN 0 00 216460 4

First published in the USA 1979
Library of Congress Catalog Card Number 78–7485–8

USA ISBN 0–529–05624–0

Set in 11 pt Monotype Baskerville

Made and printed in Great Britain by
William Collins Sons & Co. Ltd Glasgow

CONTENTS

FOREWORD

The interviews that form the subject-matter of this book took place in Recife at the end of 1975 and the beginning of 1976, between Christmas and Epiphany.

Dom Helder consented to them with his customary courtesy. In fact he didn't believe anything would come of my idea. He had greeted my request as he would greet any other: why on earth should he say no? But on the evening of the first interview, when he saw that I was serious, he became uncharacteristically anxious:

'What have I got to say that could possibly interest the world in general . . . ? I'm just an obscure Third World bishop . . . People like to come and hear my lectures because a bishop like me who talks with his hands is a curiosity. But a book is a different matter. It has to say something strong, and positive . . . And you will have to ask me questions about the past, and I have no memory for history. I'm not a historian. And neither am I a theologian; I'm not an expert in anything at all . . . No, really, I'd rather you didn't waste your time . . .'

Nevertheless he agreed to carry on: but he remained convinced that no one could ever produce a book out of the cassettes that were piling up.

Eventually Dom Helder received a copy of the edited manuscript. And his doubts and hesitation gave way to a resolution that this book must never be published. Partly because he had said too many things that he felt might damage the memory of too many people. But above all because in these impromptu memoirs where he confessed his 'errors' he found himself guilty of sharing some of the responsibility for those errors with others. How could he, Dom Helder, who is constantly appealing for understanding of human weakness, put his name to a book which pronounced or implied so many judgements on so many people? . . . It was out of the question!

The reason why the impossible became possible was that some exceptionally fine people in Brazil, whom Dom Helder has total trust in, persuaded him that his testimony was fair and that it would be productive to have it made public, even at the expense of the image of himself that he liked to cultivate and convey.

'It is another humiliation,' concluded Dom Helder, 'and I must accept it.' He is rather unlike other authors.

Since 1964 Dom Helder Camara has been Archbishop of Olinda and Recife.

Olinda stands on a hilltop, a fine colonial town, over-looking the ocean. The harbour, the docks, and the town of Recife are spread out below: it has two million inhabitants already and more every year.

Situated at the easternmost tip of Brazil, furthest outpost of the New World, Recife is the capital of the State of Pernambuco and, more importantly, of the North-East region of Brazil. The North-East is a whole country in itself. Three continents – African, European and Amerindian – join together here in an age-old struggle both for and against water and sun. The North-Easterner is a man of tempered steel.

In the 1950s, the North-East in general, and Recife in particular, became known as the 'model' of under development. Visitors are always surprised, therefore, to find Recife a busy if not prosperous metropolis. Each time I visit it there seem to be fewer and fewer poor people. Have they become richer, established, integrated?

No: they have been driven away. By sudden floods, like those of 1975 which killed several hundred people in a few hours, and which went unmentioned in the media. Or more generally, by urbanization.

You need to spend a few days with Dom Helder before you begin to glimpse, through the shiny bubble of the 'economic miracle', the other Recife and the other Brazil. His world is the world of the poor. Look through his eyes and you see how the whole order of a society that is regulated by statistics and illustrated by luxury hotels can be thrown into confusion.

Listen to his voice and you hear the security of the rich threatened by the aspirations of the poor.

History as Dom Helder sees it, lives and writes it – in an ink mixed from the mud of the Recife *alagados* – is not the history we are familiar with.

His history is about the life that continues to gush and flow under the ice.

The backdrop to our interviews in the stifling heat of a tropical summer: a frozen continent.

Superficially, order reigns in Brasilia. It is the same order as in Montevideo, Buenos Aires, Asunción, Santiago, La Paz, not to mention Lima or Quito. Order in uniform. The army is in power. The Chilean generals invented 'totalitarian democracy'. The Brazilian generals sacrifice to the god of 'national security' – even 'continental security'. The spectre of Communism has been exorcized. Capitalists need no longer fear nationalization. Tomorrow or the next day, when the energy crisis has been dealt with, when foreign importers are prepared to pay the right price for raw materials, when Brazilian investors are willing to invest at home, the economy will be able to develop and justice will emerge as a bonus. All in good time. But for the moment, order.

In Brasilia as in the rest of South America, any faction that might offer resistance, or even ask questions, has been reduced to silence, dispersed or liquidated. Workers, peasants, students, teachers, journalists and politicians must all keep in step. At the least suspicion of deviation they face arrest, prison, torture, perhaps death. No more guerrilla movements, terrorism, peasant leagues, strikes, or even demonstrations. No expression of feeling, beyond football. Businessmen may conduct their business. The United States may play at *détente* with Peking and Moscow. Security is assured.

But then there's the Church. The Church is the last remaining centre of resistance to the order that has finally been established in Brazil. Its influence is everywhere, lending support to the people, pleading on their behalf, making its voice heard. It no longer preaches patience and resignation, but campaigns for civil rights and constructs a theology of liberation. The traditional alliances have been reversed.

When peasants are thrown off land in the depths of Amazonas because it has been granted to some 'major company'; when *favelados* are evicted from their shanty huts on the outskirts of cities by bulldozers building a motorway; when a man 'disappears' from his home; when a detainee is tortured in prison: there is always a Christian who will find it out. He will carry word to his 'grass-roots community'. The 'grass-roots community' will remember the words of Christ: 'Inasmuch as ye have done it unto the least of these my brethren, ye have done it unto Me.' To do and allow to do are one and the same thing. The 'grass-roots community' won't let it happen without saying something, without doing whatever it can. It sets up a movement of protest. If it is suppressed there is always a priest who will take up the cause, then a bishop, then the regional conference of bishops, or even the national conference, either directly or through one or other of its agencies . . .

How can the country be governed, how can the order essential to national security be maintained with this constant threat of hearing the great bell toll at the slightest harm done to the meanest of citizens?

The Church must be silenced. In Brazil as in Paraguay, Argentina, Uruguay, Bolivia and Chile, the authorities are taking steps. With their armies, their police, their henchmen. Even bishops are liable to be arrested, expelled, assassinated. Paradoxically, the continent that prides itself on being the most Christian is also the one where the Church is most actively persecuted.

Dom Helder Camara, physically threatened, directly attacked through his closest friends, reduced to the state of a zombie in his own country where journalists are forbidden to mention his name, is undoubtedly not just the only, but the most eloquent witness to the monumental conflict that is taking place in Latin America between 'Christian order' and the Gospel.

Because that is what it's about. Those who have followed the course of Monsignor Lefèbvre's crusade in Europe will understand. It is no coincidence that Monsignor Lefèbvre cites Argentina and Chile as 'models' of Christian order. Why does he not mention Brazil? Here too there are generals, professors and even bishops who have committed themselves to defending the 'Eternal Church' against the subversive elements that have infiltrated its ranks. It is simply that in Brazil no one speaks of the infiltration of the Protestant ideas, or of Freemasonry, or liberalism: they speak instead of Communist infiltration.

The Church of Latin America was affected more than any other Church by the spirit of the Second Vatican Council. At the meeting of the Latin American Episcopal Council at Medellín in Colombia, with Pope Paul's blessing, it gave expression to that spirit in a form that was adapted to its own real circumstances while remaining faithful to the original. The Latin American Church rediscovered the liberating force of the Gospel. It remained only to liberate this liberating force from its institutional prison, and demonstrate it.

The Church of Latin America, more than any other Church, heard and remembered the words spoken by Paul VI as he was closing the Council: 'We too, we more than anyone else, worship man.'

In the course of its history the Church has often been persecuted for its worship of God, which pagans saw as madness. Today something else makes it suspicious and dangerous: its worship of man, which even many Christians find scandalous. Are not the two cults, like the two commandments, one and the same?

Dom Helder was known as an 'integralist' priest in the thirties, 'bishop of the slums' in the fifties, 'red bishop' today. Pope Paul VI is said to have called him 'my communist bishop'. Wherever he goes his reputation precedes him, and it is a political reputation.

This reputation does not make meeting him any less astonishing.

Dom Helder is sixty-eight. He is a frail man. The space he

occupies with his constant movement and theatrical gestures makes you forget how small he is. How does he survive the life he leads? His friends say he rarely eats a meal or has a night's sleep. But his face, his speech, his hands are imbued with remarkable energy: where does it stem from?

Like the most traditional of traditionalists, he still and always wears a cassock. A plain, black cassock. The double cuffs of his white shirt protrude slightly from the sleeves. Some years ago, in the United States, he tried wearing a dog-collar; but he decided it was not right for him and he never wore it again.

The photos taken in Rome during the Council, or later during his travels in Canada or Europe, give the impression of an eccentric individual muffled in voluminous garments like a little old man, with very unecclesiastical berets, caps or chapskas on his head. In fact these unusual accoutrements were simply necessary to protect a tropical constitution against Nordic frosts.

Nevertheless the things that have been said and written about Dom Helder's chosen poverty may have fostered a somewhat romantic image of a sort of twentieth-century Benoît Labre. It's true he sports no purple trimmings on his cassock; his pectoral cross is made of plain black wood; and the only episcopal ring he wears – and that only when he celebrates the eucharist – is the one given by Paul VI to all the Conciliar Fathers. It's true he has no car; but his friends and colleagues have cars. It's true he doesn't live in an episcopal palace; but the three rooms he has furnished in the outbuildings of a parish church are perfectly respectable. It's true he lives alone and opens his green wooden door himself to all the regular visitors, rich and poor alike, who call on him throughout the day until late at night. But he is no hermit. Dom Helder likes to relax, listen to music, join in family discussions with parents and children, and visit his friends, some of whom are rich.

More than poverty or asceticism, it is Dom Helder's simplicity that is striking. He communicates without detours. His receptiveness to everything and everybody, his ability to identify with others, no matter how remote they may seem to be from him, the deep understanding of others that he experiences and expresses make any meeting with him disturbingly like an encounter with the better part of oneself.

For a long time I wondered why the 'wise men' of Brazil persuaded Dom Helder to overcome his doubts and allow this book to be published. I concluded finally that it is because his life is characterized by an exceptional grace that lends his memoirs a universal and exemplary value.

Dom Helder has travelled straight through this century along the narrow path where history and eternity at once mingle and divide.

History is constantly present in these memoirs, as it is in Dom Helder's life. He describes his crusades alongside the Brazilian disciples of Salazar and Mussolini; he evaluates the 'revolutions' led by lieutenants, colonels, generals or guerrillas; he portrays the great men he has been close to; he devotes informed attention to popular liberation movements. His history is bound up with the history of the Brazilian giant, the Latin American powder keg, and with the defiance hurled at prosperous empires by the internationale of the oppressed.

Dom Helder is not a detached observer of the history he relates. As a young priest he 'campaigned' in the elections in his native state, Ceará. He was one of the last people to see Getúlio Vargas before he committed suicide, and later João Goulart before the 1964 landslide. He has been nominated for Mayor of Rio de Janeiro, for Federal Minister of Education, even for Vice-President of the Republic. The attack of political conscience concerning the problem of the *favelas* and the need for development planning in the regions was due partly, if not entirely, to his efforts. Like all Brazilians and South Americans he had to take sides over Fidel Castro, 'Che' Guevara and Marighela.

Although he was a friend of Camilo Torrès he himself chose the course of active non-violence – of 'pacifism' not 'passivism'. Heir to Gandhi and Martin Luther King, he has been nominated three times for the Nobel Peace Prize. It was for him that the young people of Scandinavia created the 'People's

Peace Prize'. Harvard, St Louis, the Sorbonne: the most discriminating universities have conferred on him doctorates in social sciences or law.

Eternity is more discreet. It attends the vigil which Dom Helder has devoted to prayer every night since he left the seminary. His faith irradiates his face, his words, his judgment, his decisions. It is a faith that is simple, total and free and that nourishes an indefectible hope.

It is always disturbing to meet a man possessed by a faith like this; a man who not only believes in a living, present God, but actually enacts his beliefs. The history that he relates and makes is illuminated with a strange transparency. Can things really be so simple? You feel you may be succumbing to the charms of poetry, to visions of Utopia. You have to summon all the arguments of critical reason to stop yourself tumbling into what looks like the naïvety of childhood.

It is impossible to avoid this kind of confusion with Dom Helder. Listening to or reading his words is like listening to or reading the holy scriptures: the story of a creation and a liberation which God has asked man to complete. Listening to or reading his words, you run the risk of seeing our world, today's world and tomorrow's world, through the eyes of the God of believers. It is a severe test of both reason and faith.

What have history and eternity to do with one another? At the point where they meet, the Church – all Churches – today just as twenty centuries ago, in Latin America just as all over the world, seek to define their position, their attitude and their language. What should their relation to secular powers be? What is 'Christian order'? What course can religion take that is neither alienated nor alienating?

A bishop of the Roman Catholic Church, Dom Helder Camara is primarily a churchman. He has played an important part in the Church. As an active leader of the Catholic Action movement in Brazil, he was one of the first to realize that 'the participation of the laity in the hierarchical apostolate' was merely a phase, necessary but transitory. As founder and Secretary-General for twelve years of the Brazilian National Conference of Bishops, he was one of the pioneers of episcopal collegiality, which later became the recognized mode of practice. Within the Latin American Episcopal Council, which he had helped to create, he applied himself to the work of awaking the consciousness of all the South American bishops. At the Vatican Council, where he made no public contribution, he was the kingpin of the 'Church of the Poor' group, and above all, of the 'Friday meetings of Vatican II' which had traced the monumental John XXIII's great enterprise.

Now, in the post-Council crisis, when the Church is divided into obstreperous and jealous camps, Dom Helder is unclassifiable: on neither one side nor the other, neither on the fence, nor in the midst, nor remote. Capable of dialogue with everyone, he is a challenge to all. In fact, the sovereign liberty in which he practises his faith is something of an embarrassment to all. Perhaps this is why he is not a cardinal, rather than for the reasons of political prudence generally supposed.

From one error to another, he confesses, Dom Helder's itinerary is made up of a succession of conversions, and it is not yet ended. Conversion under the guidance of the Holy Spirit is, for the Archbishop of Recife, the only way of being faithful. A marked contrast to those 'faithful' that cling fast to tradition, or prostitute themselves to fashion.

One more comment to end this foreword. A comment made by my neighbour in the Boeing which took me back from Recife to Paris via Lisbon. He had seen me talking to Dom Helder at the airport, exchanging a final *abraço*:

'That man is dangerous.'

The door of the aeroplane had just closed. My neighbour was determined to get things straight. He had let me know where he stood, and he was waiting for me to do the same.

For a moment I experienced the temptation that prompted Saint Peter to deny, perfectly naturally, that he had anything to do with this Jesus of Nazareth who had just been arrested. Just because they had been seen together once or twice . . .

In his artful, polite challenge I sensed almost a wink of connivance: 'You know, despite the way it looks, I am quite prepared to believe that you have nothing to do with him.' Ever since Judas we have known that an *abraço* doesn't make a disciple.

My neighbour was a Portuguese businessman. He had set up business in Brazil, and was doing well. He was a reasonable man. Getting into the aeroplane I had returned to the world of serious people. Never before have I experienced this physical sensation of moving from one universe to another.

Under my seat were eighteen hours or so of taped conversations with 'that man', whom I could not bring myself to find 'dangerous'. All through the long Atlantic night a jumble of his words, phrases, anecdotes and ideas haunted me. I should have liked to let my neighbour hear them. Not to reassure him, but to have helped him realize that the real dangers are perhaps not where he imagines. I dedicate this book to him, on behalf of Dom Helder.

José de Broucker

I

WE CEARANS

*You were born in Fortaleza, the capital of the state
of Ceará, in the North-East of Brazil. Tell us a little
bit about your home town – about Fortaleza as you
knew it, and as it is today.*

At the beginning of the century Fortaleza was just a provincial town. Today it has a million inhabitants. But even in
those days it had a rather urban look about it, with wide
straight streets, almost like avenues. I think it was designed
by some former mayor who liked making plans.

But at that time the town lacked many things. There was
no electricity, for one thing. That wasn't surprising. And
there was no water in the houses.

You got it from a pump?

No: when I was a child little donkeys went about the streets
carrying water, or sometimes wood. This was because we
didn't have any gas in the houses either, and everyone –
particularly the poor people – had to buy wood for fires and
for cooking. There were also no sewers. Each family had its
own cesspit.

However, one by one the first multi-storey buildings – sky-
scrapers – began to appear, and the first motor cars. It
wasn't like today, when you can hardly walk anywhere in
Fortaleza because of the traffic. This was the beginning of
motorized transport. I remember the first aeroplanes, too. It
used to be a great event, in the early days, when an aeroplane

went over: everyone ran outside and stared.

Today the most striking thing about Fortaleza is the contrast between the very, very rich houses – too rich – as big as cinemas or nightclubs, and beside them, right next to them, the most dreadful poverty. I know there are contrasts everywhere. I know that every rich country has certain grey areas of slums. But nowadays in Fortaleza, and every day increasingly so – in my day it wasn't so noticeable – the contrasts have become really shocking.

When was Fortaleza founded?

It isn't as old as Olinda, for instance. But it was originally the 'Fortress' (Fortaleza) of Our Lady of the Assumption. There are many towns like that, whose names have lost their meaning: like San Francisco in California – Saint Francis of California. And São Paulo: people forget that the founders named it after the apostle Paul.

Today Fortaleza is a modern city.

Industrial?

Yes, to some extent. But the industrialization of the North-East is another story altogether.

You lived in Fortaleza for twenty-seven years. Are you still attached to it? Do you still feel homesick?

Well, Fortaleza is the capital of Ceará. And we Cearans are devoted to our homeland.

What is Ceará like? And what is a Cearan like?

Well, first let me explain that Brazil is divided into regions, like a microcosm of the world. We have the South, which is more or less developed, especially around São Paulo, and we have Amazonia, the North, the Central-West, the South-East, and the North-East. And within the North-East is the state of Ceará.

The thing that characterizes Ceará – and this is still true today, although less so than in the past – is drought. Not through lack of water: there is rain. But through the irregularity of the rainfall. Sometimes there's a deluge that can last a week or two. And then a week, a month, a year, three years, go by without a drop of rain. It's disastrous. The trees lose all their leaves and, of course, stop bearing fruit. The rivers dry up completely. Animals become too weak to move: they simply die in their tracks. And the people have to go away.

Of course a lot of work is being done now to minimize the effects of drought – irrigation and so on. But in the meantime – without going into the complex problems of the North-East – what happens is that frequently Cearans are forced to leave their homes. They have always had to leave because of droughts, and now they have to leave for other reasons as well, social reasons. Most of them go south, to São Paulo, or Paraná. Or they go to Amazonia. Amazonia has always played an important part in the Cearan imagination. But as soon as the rain comes, as soon as winter comes, all they can think of is collecting their belongings and going back to Ceará.

There's a story – maybe it's true – about someone who arrived in Heaven and was shocked to see a man in chains. Naturally he said to Saint Peter: 'What's this? It's impossible! Are there prisons in Heaven? Men in chains?' And Saint Peter said: 'No, he's a Cearan. He found out that it's winter time in Ceará, and if we don't tie him up, he escapes!' Even from Heaven, imagine that!

Cearans are travellers. You meet them everywhere. In São Paulo there are more Cearans than any other North-Easterners. You even meet them abroad.

North-Easterners in general, including Cearans, are short, dark-haired people. Even if they don't have the opportunity to study or get professional training, they have a remarkable practical intelligence. In Rio de Janeiro, for instance, and in São Paulo, I've often come across Cearans who have never been trained to work in radio or television, but have suddenly, overnight, become experts in this area.

North-Easterners are also very courageous when it comes to suffering or difficulties, or hard work. We're not a lazy people, I can assure you. Perhaps that is our response to nature, which demands more of us than it gives.

But how can you love Ceará, if it's like you describe it?

It's very easy to love your mother if she is beautiful and intelligent. But when you are her son, and she is your mother, beauty and intelligence don't determine whether you love her or not. Your heart decides. Ceará is our land, our mother: we belong to her! We can't help it! But there are other, more profound reasons, many of them subconscious, no doubt. Fundamentally we realize that God has bestowed on mankind not only the right but also the duty to subdue nature and complete the work of creation. I think Cearans instinctively know that they can't blame God for the droughts and the floods. It's true there are still prayers and hymns and processions asking Him to solve the problem. But I think this love of the homeland expresses, subconsciously, the conviction that it is up to us to control the droughts and floods. It isn't God's problem. It would be so easy for Him to create perfect, finished worlds! But think how monotonous that would be! I much prefer to have a task set before me. And if we haven't yet managed to overcome the droughts and the floods, it is our fault, our sin.

Cearans have many virtues. Have they no vices?

A certain vanity, a certain pride. Do you know what a *jangada* is? It's a primitive boat that the fishermen build here on the coast. Three planks and a sail. The story goes that one day two Cearans set sail in one of these little boats, and made for the open sea. A great transatlantic liner was going past. One of the liner's crew caught sight of the *jangada* through his telescope, and told the captain. The captain gave the order to slow down and signal. So one of the *jangadeiros* said to the other: 'What's the matter? Do they need help?' I love telling these stories. But that's what Cearan pride is like.

Pride, yes, but lack of awareness too, perhaps?

Yes, if you like. Their courage is unconscious: but they seem to perform miracles. They have absolutely no life-saving equipment, yet they go fishing right out into deep waters. It isn't like having a boat fitted with a motor and radar and so on.

But obviously we have weaknesses: vanity, and pride . . . I once saw a very short Cearan talking to a tall man. The tall man was trying to make fun of him, but the little Cearan said: 'Listen! Height doesn't prove anything. You measure a man from here up!' And he pointed to his eyes.

Have Fortaleza and Ceará produced any famous people?

Yes indeed, and we're very proud of them. People who helped to abolish slavery, for instance. Brazil, as you know, still imported African slaves until 1888. It was terrible. Boatloads of slaves . . .

But surely importing slaves was prohibited long before 1888?

Yes, but it still went on secretly. And when the slaves were brought ashore they separated husbands from wives and children from parents. It was horrible. But here in Ceará we put an end to it long before the rest of Brazil.

Whose decision was that?

The people decided. The people forced the government to act. One day Nascimento, the leader of the *jangadeiros* of Fortaleza, simply said: 'No more slaves will ever be landed at this port.' And they never were. The people who were campaigning to abolish slavery in Brazil called Ceará 'the land of light', *Terra da luz*. We Cearans were very proud. Slavery is still a disgrace to us all, but at least we can take comfort in what happened here then.

There must have been slave-owners in Ceará, like everywhere else. Did they accept the decision?

Well, it only stopped them landing more slaves – it didn't mean they had to release the ones who were already here. But it was at least a gesture which expressed the will of the

people. Of course, it was a different matter with the owners
and the bosses.

Other famous Cearans are the jurist Clovis Bevilacqua, the
historian Capistrano de Abreu, and the novelist José de
Alencar – one of the creators of Brazilian romanticism. He
wrote about the native people in a poetic style. His hero,
Peri, is the ideal noble Indian – unfortunately far removed
from the sad reality of the Brazilian Indians. You see we've
never had Indians like the Aztecs, or the Incas, or the Mayas.
But de Alencar's vision of the Indians expressed our people's
secret desire for such a heritage. Iracema . . . she was another
of his characters. Cearans consider the Indians their an-
cestors, as well as the Portuguese.

The black population of Ceará is quite small, isn't
it?

I wouldn't say it's small; but it's smaller than in other parts
of Brazil. One of the unusual things about the North-East is
that there are so few foreign immigrants. In the South there
are a great many Italians, Germans, Japanese . . . But in the
North-East in general, and in Ceará in particular, nearly
everyone is of Portuguese descent.

But there were some Dutch immigrants, weren't
there?

Yes, here and there you come across blond Cearans, and
people always say, in a mocking sort of way, they must be
Dutch. But in terms of numbers, they are negligible.

Was there a large Indian population?

Yes, although not as large as in Bolivia, or Paraguay.

Would it be true to say that the North-Eastern
Indians have been wiped out?

Well, you see . . . in Brazil, in addition to the Negro problem,
there were also Indian slaves. But I think José de Alencar's
glorification and romanticization of the native Indians to

some extent expresses our view of them. We are glad to be descended from both the Portuguese and the Indians.

Slave and master all in one?

Since you put it like that, perhaps I should begin to explain that unfortunately in the poorer, less developed areas of Brazil slavery still exists. Of course, it hasn't been official since 1888. But there are still groups of rich people who maintain their wealth at the expense of their fellow citizens, condemning them to live in misery, in sub-human conditions. That is slavery. And when you look at the regions that produce raw materials – rubber, sugar cane, cocoa, coffee – you realize that they are still suffering from what the Church, in Medellín, has called internal colonialism. But the worst thing of all was the blindness of the people. And particularly our blindness, the blindness of the Church. I'm not passing judgement. It's impossible, unfair, to judge the past by present standards. But our obsession with maintaining the social order prevented us from seeing the terrible injustice that was hidden, and still is hidden today, within that order. The Christianity we preached was too passive. I say this because you brought up the question of our dual heritage – masters and slaves, conquerors and conquered.

As a North-Easterner and a Cearan, do you personally feel that you belong more to the masters of Brazil, or the slaves?

I'm afraid that when I was young, when I was in the seminary and even after I became a priest I suffered from the general blindness. It took time, a great deal of time, in fact, before my eyes began to open – always supposing that they are really open now. It's terrible to realize how, even in the midst of so much suffering, the concern to maintain authority and order prevented us from discovering and denouncing injustice. Our job was to preach patience, obedience and the acceptance of suffering in union with Christ. Great virtues, no doubt. But in that context we were simply tools of the authorities: so yes, we were on the side of the

masters. Until the time when the Church refused to go on
supporting established injustices, and internal colonialism:
when we realized that it was our duty to denounce injustice
and to dedicate ourselves to the advancement of the people.
It caused a great scandal. But you know what happened . . .

> Obviously we'll come back to this during the course
> of our discussions. But for the moment let's come
> back to Ceará. Is there a kind of solidarity among
> Cearans when they meet in Rio de Janeiro, or São
> Paulo, or elsewhere? A family feeling?

I don't want to idealize Cearans: we have the same capacity
for selfishness as everyone else. But suffering does tend to
bring us together. Very often suffering creates solidarity. For
example, if a mother dies leaving young children, it's very
common to see another woman who already has about ten
children of her own taking in these other children to look
after them.

Our people have their own way of looking at God and
men. They recognize immediately a man who has a heart,
who is compassionate and sensitive, and concerned about
others. They will respect him at once and will venerate him
almost like a saint.

Take Father Cicero, for instance, who was so popular. It's
quite easy to become a Father Cicero.

> Easy – in Ceará?

Not just in Ceará, but all over the world, it seems to me.
Certainly in Brazil the people are particularly sensitive to
goodness. Father Cicero was a profoundly humane person.
Above all, he loved the poor. He went about and talked to
the people: he was respected and loved. More than that,
even. While he was still alive he was truly venerated. Adored.

I knew him, I met him. I was very young at the time, and
he was very old. He taught me a lesson, in fact, which I have
never forgotten.

When I was in the seminary I went to Joazeiro to publicize our diocesan newspaper, *O Nordeste*. I needed Father
Cicero's support. When I went to see him he said to me: 'In

worldly terms I see no reason why I should help your news-paper. It attacks me viciously without ever sending a reporter to interview me, or giving me the chance to defend myself. But you are a young seminarist. Soon you will be a priest. And I have to prove to you, not just in words but in deeds, that there must be no room for a single drop of hatred in the heart of a Christian, least of all a priest.' And he gave me his support. I came back to Fortaleza loaded down with sub-scriptions.

All my life I have remembered this lesson in Christian generosity. And now that what was happening to him then is happening to me, on a larger scale, God is helping me to live out the words of Father Cicero: 'not even a single drop of hatred in the heart of a priest.'

Another example is Brother Damião. He's still alive; but he's become as famous in his own lifetime as Father Cicero became after his death.

> In Ceará?

No, not just in Ceará, but all over the North-East. Brother Damião is an Italian. He came here as a missionary when he was very young, almost forty years ago. I go to hear him myself, sometimes. Often you can't understand a word he says, but that doesn't matter. It's enough just to see him and touch him. We love people who are good, who are full of warmth and understanding.

> How are the goodness and warmth and understand-ing of someone like Brother Damião expressed? How do people know he has those qualities?

Oh, they can tell! They have antennae. They feel it. They have an instinct for people who are really receptive, ready to understand. In fact it's curious, because Brother Damião's religion, his morality, is very harsh and extreme. In his sermons he condemns modern fashions – although I've told him these people are too poor even to be tempted by the fashions. But it doesn't matter. They know that Brother Damião prays for them all. He suffers with everyone who is suffering.

I think Cearans also have a particular capacity for adapting to new circumstances, to all sorts of strange situations and foreign climates. They seem to have a sense of the universal, without ever losing their essential North-Eastern, Cearan character.

Most Cearans, especially the poor people, sleep in hammocks. For us a hammock is a symbol. Very often it is a bridal bed for married couples. For babies it is a cradle; for children it is a kind of space ship: we play in it, and swing and fly, and our imaginations carry us higher and higher, towards the stars. When we are ill, it is a sick bed. When we have to carry a sick person it becomes a stretcher. And when poor people die, if they can't afford a coffin, they are buried in a hammock.

If a Cearan sees a hammock in Europe, or Australia, or Japan, or anywhere else, he will be deeply moved, as if he had come across a little bit of his homeland.

> You were born in 1909. What was Brazil like at the beginning of the century?

It was known as a predominantly agricultural country at that time. And it was agricultural: but in the worst sense of the word. It was true that the majority of the population worked on the land; but they lived in sub-human conditions. And those conditions have never been radically reformed.

Now the countryside is being taken over by huge companies. They move into a new area and form alliances with the local privileged class. And the *campesinos*, the agricultural workers, are forced to move out, displaced by new methods of cultivation or husbandry. Their families may have been there for decades, but very often they have no deeds, no documents, no pieces of paper. They simply have to leave. So they make for the towns. The towns get bigger, but their expansion is like a cancer. The poor people think that if they go to the towns they will find work, and schools, and hospitals. But when they arrive they find there isn't even anywhere for them to live, except in the most impossible places – on river banks, or beside the sea.

At the turn of the century, Brazil was a predominantly

agricultural country. But it was the agriculture of the poor. They used the same wretched methods of farming that had been handed down from the Portuguese, or from the Indians, or the Africans. And of course the results were wretched too.

> Were they growing cotton, sugar cane and coffee then?

Yes. In fact the North-East, particularly Pernambuco, enjoyed a period of great prosperity. In the early days, the land was the chief source of wealth as it produced sugar cane. But as you know, there's a tragic story behind every raw material. The prices are fixed elsewhere, in the great trading centres – and today, by multinational companies. It's very easy for us Brazilians to understand what happened to Chilean copper, because it happened to our Amazonian rubber, to our North-Eastern cotton, to our sugar cane, and to our coffee.

> In 1909 the Republic was less than twenty years old.

You know, a Republic, a First Republic, a Second Republic, or an Empire, doesn't make much difference to an oppressed people. It still means misery and exploitation. Neither the Empire nor the Republic managed to create a fairer social structure in Brazil. The only difference was the colour of the flag or the names of the parties. The people who come to power – executive, legislative, and judicial power – are always members of the privileged classes. Because the elections – especially in those days when voting was not secret – were organized in such a way that you had to vote the way your employer wanted you to. Later they tried to make elections fairer, with secret ballots and electoral courts: but in general, especially in rural areas, voters are still under very strong pressures.

> But you must have been taught, at school and at home, that you were living in a Republic, and not an Empire any longer? Were you glad?

Yes – but we always had a soft spot for the Emperor. He was a nice man. People never forgot what Pedro II once said when there was a drought in Ceará: 'I will sell the last jewel from my crown rather than let a single Cearan die of hunger!'

But, as I said, as far as the people were concerned, living under an Empire or a Republic didn't make any difference.

> In Fortaleza, in Ceará, did you regard Brazil as a single nation? Did Rio de Janeiro not seem to you a very remote capital?

No. We were very much aware of being a single nation. Our national consciousness is a legacy from the Portuguese. It is a vast country, as big as a continent, but we all speak the same language. There are no dialects. We all share the Christian faith. We all feel Brazilian. Of course there are tremendous regional differences. At first Pernambuco was the richest area. Then the South developed rapidly, at the expense of the North-East. The profits from our raw materials were used to finance industrial expansion in São Paulo. But it didn't stop people feeling that they all belonged to the same country. We were even a little proud to see the industry developing in the South. But in fact these regional differences and the unequal distribution of development caused severe problems. More recently attempts are being made to even out the discrepancies – by developing the North-East, for example.

> Very often children are told stories about their country's enemies, to make them patriotic. Who are Brazil's traditional enemies?

To be honest, with our history we have no right to condemn North American imperialism today. When the world was divided into spheres of influence determined by the Popes instead of the Great Powers, Latin America was divided by the Tordesillas line. But Brazil expanded far beyond that line: the *bandeirantes* were constantly looking further afield for gold, driving out the Indians as they went. Brazil annexed Uruguay twice. Then later we joined forces

with Uruguay and Argentina to attack Paraguay, claiming
that it was planning to attack Brazil. For the next five years
we proceeded to devastate Paraguay. When I was a child,
people described the war with Paraguay as glorious and
patriotic, and even today they still celebrate its anniversaries.
But I think you Europeans also kept alive the memory of
your fratricidal wars for a long time. Until you finally
realized that it is not the best way to write history.

> When you were a child, I suppose the greatest power
> Brazil had to contend with was Great Britain?

Wealthy families were most influenced by France: they
adopted French customs and bought French goods. If they
drank mineral water, it was Vichy water; if they drank
champagne, it was Veuve Cliquot! But the great power, the
empire of the day, was indeed Great Britain. The queen of
the seas. She controlled our railways, the North-West, and
our exports, particularly cotton. That was until the Second
World War – and then there was a new empire. The
United States took over from Great Britain. I am always
struck by the fact that history is a succession of empires. I
dream of the day when instead of worrying about which
empire will be next we can all look forward to a new age, an
age without empires.

2

MOTHER AND FATHER:
TEACHER AND FREEMASON

> You were born into a fairly middle-class, well-educated family: I imagine it was not during your childhood that you first got to know of the poverty that was to have such a great influence on you later in life. Your father was a businessman: what line of business was he in?

He worked for a trading company. He was a book-keeper. In those days it was called a *guarda libros*. The company was called Boris Brothers. Monsieur Boris was a French Jew. My father never earned very much. His job was very humble. But when he retired, after thirty-five years, the house that he had rented from Boris Brothers was given to him.

My father and mother between them earned just enough to pay for necessities. I remember more than once my mother gathered us all together and said: 'We have to do without something for a while.' Sometimes it would be butter, sometimes dessert.

My parents had an absolute horror of debt. We had to live on what they earned, and no more. There was no question of any luxuries.

> No holidays, I suppose – no travelling?

The first time I ever rode in a motor car was when one of my brothers got married. It was a great event! We hired a taxi to take us to church, and all the neighbours came out to watch.

When I went into a seminary my parents couldn't afford the full fees, they could only pay about half.

How many brothers and sisters did you have?

Well, my parents had thirteen children altogether. But five of them died very young in a croup epidemic.

And your mother was a teacher in a state school?

Yes, but in rather unusual circumstances. In those days the State couldn't afford to build as many schools as were needed, so classes were often held in private houses. That was what happened at our house. My mother was paid her teacher's salary, and then an allowance to pay part of the rent of our house, where she gave her lessons.

I can still see her now, in the big classroom. I have so many memories of her. Whenever I think of injustice, I remember my mother. She felt that her own children should set an example to the rest: so she was very strict with us. One day when I was little she set me a task which was really too difficult for me. I couldn't solve the problem, and burst into tears. My mother stood up abruptly, and I thought she was going to cane me – even though she never had before. But instead she handed me a little picture with an inscription: 'To my son, of whom I ask too much.'

My mother helped me enormously. She came from the Cearan hinterland region of Upper Sertão. She was born during the great drought of 1877 and her family was forced to leave their home when she was two or three, to escape starvation. She went to the teachers' training college in Fortaleza, and became a schoolteacher.

She taught me a great deal. I remember one day when we were talking she pointed to her face (she often spoke with her hands) and said to me: 'When you are older, many people will tell you that this was created by God, this – ' pointing to her bosom – 'by who knows what, and the rest – ' indicating the rest of her body – 'by the devil. But it isn't true, my son! From your head to your toes, you are God's creature!' I was five years old at the time, but her words made a great impression on me. And I think that incident will give you an idea of how unconventional her views were, at a time when it was normal to look for sin everywhere.

> I was going to ask what sort of religious upbringing you had, but your story has already answered the question.

At that time, it seemed as if even God must spend all His time sniffing out sins, counting them, classifying them, taking notes! Everything was bad, everything was sinful, especially sex. But the things my mother taught me – and I could tell you other stories like this one – were completely different: she had a totally different attitude. I am very grateful to the Lord for giving me a mother who could teach me not only Portuguese, basic mathematics, geography and history, but also lessons in life.

> Was it not a privilege, at that time, to be able to go to school?

School attendance was compulsory, by law. But the government didn't have the means to offer every child the real opportunity of going to school. In that sense, it was a privilege.

The story about my mother reminds me of my seminary, where I met men who shared her broad vision of life. I remember one day, for example, I said to one of my teachers: 'Father, how can you explain the fact that God, who is Love, has imposed on us ten commandments which are all negative? Thou shalt not, thou shalt not, thou shalt not: all negative. I could understand if it were in the Old Testament. But Christ said He had not come to change the Law.' And the priest, who was a Dutchman, replied: 'When Christ was asked what was the first commandment, he replied categorically: "Thou shalt love the Lord thy God with all thy heart, and with all thy soul, and with all thy mind; and thy neighbour as thyself." And He added that these two commandments embraced both the Law and the Prophets.' You see! It is a positive vision! And anyone who passes through this life obeying those two commandments, loving God and loving his neighbour, will have the joy of being received by the Lord!

> Your father was a freemason. What did it mean, exactly, to be a freemason in Brazil at the turn of the century?

I think the reason my father, and his father, his brothers, and all the rest of the family, became freemasons was because they were anti-clerical, rather than anti-religious or even, as I will show you, anti-Christian. It wasn't even that they were opposed to 'true' priests. It seemed to me then, and still seems to me now, that they were reacting against some of the Church's attitudes, and also, perhaps, against certain individual priests.

Although my father was a freemason he was not by any means anti-religious. For example, all through my childhood he observed a tradition which he had inherited from his father. In our house there was a little wooden sanctuary. I remember it had a large crucifix – Christ on the cross, but without the cross. There was a Virgin Mary, and Saint Francis of Assisi. And every day throughout the month of May, from the first to the thirty-first, my father would call all the family together and recite the Rosary. Then he sang the Litany of Our Lady in Latin. Of course he had the text in front of him. But he always sang the litanies. And finally we always sang a hymn in honour of the Virgin. May was always a holy month for us.

So here was this man, a freemason, who wore on his hand a ring inscribed with the symbol of freemasonry, for whom God was more than just the Grand Architect, honouring the Virgin Mary – praying to her with all his heart all through every month of May: 'Mother of God, Mother of God, pray for us, miserable sinners . . .' All the Christian mysteries are there: creation, incarnation, sin, salvation.

As I said, my father was not opposed to the Church, nor to true priests. I don't remember the first time I said that I wanted to become a priest: I may have been three or four. But one day, when I was older, my father said to me: 'Son, you are always saying that you want to be a priest. But do you really know what that means? Do you know that if you are a priest you cannot be selfish? To be a priest and selfish is impossible. The two things don't go together. You cannot be a priest and remain selfish.' He went on, expounding to me his vision of priesthood, and of the Eucharist: 'Priests believe that when they administer the Eucharist, it is the body of Christ Himself. So have you thought about how pure those hands must be, if they actually touch Christ?' Of course, I was enthralled. He was saying exactly what I had been feeling, perhaps unconsciously, in the depths of my soul.

And when he had finished his portrait of a priest, I said to him: 'Father, that's exactly the kind of priest I want to be.' And he replied: 'Then may God bless you, my son. God bless you. You know we haven't very much money, but never mind, we'll see how we can help you get into a seminary.'

> Were there any echoes in your family of the 'religious question' of the 1870s, when the Church and State in Brazil clashed violently over freemasonry?

No, not really. My grandfather was the editor of a newspaper in Fortaleza, *A Republica*: but I never really had a chance to read it because by the time I was old enough to understand my grandfather was dead and the paper no longer existed.

I'm sure that in Fortaleza, as elsewhere, the freemasons followed the 'religious question' closely. But I have the feeling that the freemasons condemned by Dom Vital, the Archbishop of Recife at the time of the controversy, were not really anti-religious, nor exactly anti-Christian, nor even anti-Church, but perhaps simply opposed to certain abuses within the Church, and what they felt to be the Church's interference in the secular domain. At least that is how it was seen in my family.

One of my sisters – she's dead now – was going to become a nun, and she asked my father to give up freemasonry. That wasn't surprising in those days; but my father was very hurt. He said to her: 'My dear girl, of course I want to receive the sacraments. I have no difficulty with the Creed: I say it often, I know it by heart. But to give up freemasonry would mean betraying the memory of my father and the rest of my family. I assure you, the freemasons have never taught me anything against God or the Church or any heresy. Never.'

Fortunately our priest was very understanding and appreciated my father's feelings. He said to him: 'There is no need for you to reject freemasonry if it has been your way of life. All you need to do is say the Creed with all your heart.'

> You mentioned that your grandfather was a newspaper editor. Your father was also a journalist for a time – a critic, if I remember rightly. And your uncle was a playwright. And of course one of your brothers gained a certain notoriety as a literary critic. That's a lot of men of letters for one family. Have you ever been tempted to write and publish your ideas? And is it because of this family tradition that you are so at ease with people who work in the press, radio and television, and in the theatre and music?

My father was mainly a theatre critic. At that time, the only theatrical performances in Fortaleza were given by a few visiting companies; but my father was passionately enthusiastic about every performance. He analysed the plays very acutely. Sometimes he used to take us to the theatre with him. He got free tickets because he was a critic. And sometimes he used to read plays to us. He read very well, with fire and feeling. Or he sang to us. I remember his voice vividly.

> Did he sing folk songs?

No, usually it was pieces from opera, classical pieces. My brother, the one who was a literary critic, used to get all sorts of new books sent to him – Brazilian and French. He also read very well: with intelligence, and warmth. He had a great influence on my reading. In a way he played a part in my ... well, no, I can't say my literary vocation, that would be going too far. But certainly he awakened and encouraged my taste for literature. He introduced me to classical Brazilian literature – but he also helped me to read and appreciate modern works. He introduced me to French literature as well.

Which of the things you read impressed you most?

While I was under the influence of my brother Gilbert, our literary guide was *Le Figaro*. And I read practically the entire works of Sainte-Beuve, whom my brother regarded as the model critic.

Later, in Rio de Janeiro, I went through a Claudel phase: *l'Annonce faite à Marie*, *l'Otage*, *les Odes*. Claudel, mixed with Péguy, and Saint-Exupéry. Later still I discovered *le Milieu divin* and *la Messe sur le Monde*, and was surprised and delighted to find myself a devotee of Teilhard de Chardin.

Were there many students of European literature in Fortaleza at that time?

There have always been groups of avid readers in the North-Eastern towns. They have a greater aptitude for reading than people in the big cities, where there are too many other things to do and see, and where people have neither the time, nor perhaps the inclination.

And it was French literature that they read, rather than British or American?

French literature. My brother didn't read English. It was easier for us to learn French: it was more prevalent in my day.

Even during the First World War? Do you remember the war? Perhaps you were too young?

Not at all! I remember it very well. As my father's boss was a Frenchman, he used to get newspapers and magazines with photographs of the war. I followed it with a passionate interest: I was on the side of France. And we read other French newspapers.

But we were talking about the theatre. It wasn't only the spectacle or the actual performance that fascinated me: when my uncle, Carlos Camara, wrote a new play, I used to love to go to rehearsals. I loved to watch the play emerging for the first time. The author would also direct the play: he chose the cast; and he was furious if one of the actors didn't perform a role as he had conceived it. He would take the actor's place, and give the speech himself, and say: 'You see! That is how it must be!' To me that was far more exciting than the play itself.

> The artist's involvement in his work?

The sense of creation. It was thrilling to watch this man who had written the play now setting it in motion, giving it life.

> Were you thinking of your uncle later, when you directed paraliturgical plays in the stadium at Rio de Janeiro?

Perhaps, subconsciously – all these things leave an impression. But in the seminary I had another encounter which was very important in my . . . literary life, if you like. With my second Rector.

My first Rector was a Dutchman, Guilherme Vassen. He was really a missionary. We respected him enormously: and I remember vividly how inspired I felt the day he announced that he was resigning from the seminary to pursue his vocation as a missionary. I was called upon to say goodbye to him on behalf of all the seminarists. I remember what I said. I was just an adolescent. 'Go, Father: your sons will watch you go as the sons of the Crusaders watched their fathers go. We shall be with you in spirit.' It was something like that, really adolescent.

My second Rector was a Frenchman, Tobie Dequidt. I got on well with him, and we talked about all sorts of things. For example, I remember that even in the senior seminary every pupil had a desk with a padlock, and the padlock had two keys: one for the seminarist, and one for the Rector.

One morning when I went to collect my prayer books from my desk as usual before six o'clock mass – the first missals in Latin were just beginning to circulate – my neighbour said to me: 'The Rector says that if you notice something missing from your desk you should go and fetch it from him.' When I opened my desk I found everything upside down. I didn't even bother to look, I just closed it again and went to mass.

A week went by, and then another, and still I didn't go to the Rector. But one day I happened to meet him in the corridor, and he said: 'Well, don't you want your papers?' 'Sir, may I speak frankly?' 'Of course!' 'As you know, I love you and respect you very much, both as a teacher and as a friend. And so I prefer to lose my papers rather than come and ask you for them: because I am sure you would be ashamed to admit that you went into our classroom in the middle of the night like a thief, and opened my desk, and looked through my things. I cannot bear to submit you to such humiliation.'

By now he was trembling with emotion. I had touched him deeply. 'Yes, yes! You – you are right! It *is* shameful. I should never have done it! I shall never do it again!' He went on and on. 'But you see, my son, there were these poems in your desk!' 'Rector, surely you don't condemn poetry, when you are a poet yourself?' 'How do you know that I am a poet?' 'Because whenever you read a beautiful line, a strong line, or when you see something beautiful in nature, you seem to come to life. You can't help it! I can tell that you are a poet! So I repeat, will you condemn poetry when you are a poet yourself?' 'But that's exactly why I must do it! I see you as a priest: I sense that you have a vocation, and I know the dangers poetry led me into. I want to protect you from them: from your imagination!' 'Sir, forgive me! But imagination is the gift of God! In my family, when we want to describe someone who has no personality or intelligence, we say that he has no imagination! It's terrible, to us, to say that someone has no imagination: because imagining is a way of participating in the creative power of the Lord. How can you be afraid of that? How can you be opposed to imagination? It is a gift of God!' 'But my son, poetry takes us so far, so much further than we may want to go!' 'Sir, you are very fair with me:

you haven't convinced me at all, but you don't *pretend* that you have convinced me, either. So let's make a pact. I promise that until I am ordained I will give up what you call my poems, and what I call my meditations. But you must trust me, and never search my desk again. For my own part, I swear: no more poetry until I'm a priest.'

And was the pact kept?

Yes, absolutely. As I left the Rector that day I noticed that he had tears in his eyes. I remember he said to me: 'For a time, you are giving up poetry. But it isn't the end. Here in Brazil we have no winter, we never see snow. But if you were in Europe and you saw snow, it would be naive to think that it presaged death. Instead, it prepares the way for spring. You will see.' This was the poet in him speaking.

So that was how I talked to my Rector.

I remember another incident involving him. I'd like to tell you about it – though I haven't forgotten that you asked me originally about my literary influences. I'll come back to that.

One day this Rector, Father Tobie Dequidt, sent for me and said: 'I have some good news for you. You are to be admitted to the tonsure – the first step towards ordination.' I was delighted, and said: 'Then I have a request, sir.' 'I know, you would like a day's holiday, I expect? And not just for yourself, I'm sure: you'd like everyone to have a holiday?' 'No, not at all.' 'Then perhaps you would like to be allowed to talk in the refectory?' 'No, really, that isn't it. It's something far more important than that.' 'What, then?' 'Rector, since you are prepared to admit me to the path of the priesthood, without any special merit on my part, I think you should also be able to accept my application to join the Children of Mary. Do you realize, sir, that every semester since I entered the seminary I have applied to be admitted to the Children of Mary, and every time my application is turned down. Why? Because, sir, there are certain prohibitions in this seminary which make no sense. Let me give you an example. We are supposed to observe silence in all the corridors. Well, it's easy enough to force people to be silent: far easier than getting them to talk to one another with respect and consideration, like human beings. But I'm too young to understand that, and so I rebel and talk. And if I see a teacher coming along the corridor, I carry on talking. It seems to me it's a question of honour, a test of character. Obviously it earns me a black mark, so I'm refused entry to the Children of Mary. And then there's the study room: we're supposed to be silent there, too. We're forbidden to consult or help our neighbours. In other words we are being taught to enclose ourselves in selfishness, in individualism. Is that the way to teach us to be priests? Surely not: so I rebel in the study room as well. I talk, I consult my friends when I need to, and I help them when I can. If the teacher on duty looks at me, I carry on talking deliberately: it is a matter of honour. And that means another black mark, and another rejection from the Children of Mary.'

And the Rector replied: 'My son, you shall be admitted to the Children of Mary this very day.' But I said: 'Sir, you may think you have already granted me too great a favour: but I'm afraid I cannot agree to be admitted alone. At least eighteen of my friends are in exactly the same position.' And he said: 'All of them, if they wish, may be admitted to the Children of Mary tomorrow.'

He was a very intelligent, honourable man, this Rector. He knew how to accept criticism, and recognize injustice. He was genuinely prepared to discuss things. The next day I went to thank him, and said: 'Rector, I have yet another request. Will you try an experiment? In my class there are some boys who need extra help with their work, and others who understand more quickly and are further ahead with their lessons. Why not let those who prefer to work in silence remain in the study room, while the others go into another room to work together? I think those who are more able – not on their own merits, but because they have received this gift from God – ought to share their ability. For instance, my friend Luis Braga could easily help to teach science; and I could help with philosophy. And then he could teach ethics, and I could take dogma.'

It was a way of sharing. The Rector agreed to the experiment, and it was continued even after I left the seminary.

But to return to literature. This Rector, with whom I had the conversation about poetry, used to get many books sent to him, including French ones. He gave me the task of opening the parcels and slitting the pages; and he also let me read the books. It meant that I was able to observe and share in his preferences. I saw, for instance, that in his youth he had followed Marc Sangnier: he had been a Sillonist. He had been inspired by that philosophy. And I remember when he received Blondel's *l'Action*, which the Holy Office already considered suspect.

But one day he handed me a book which had several pages clipped together. 'Cut this book, and read it, but not those pages.' And I said: 'I'm sorry, sir, but I would rather not take the book at all if you can't trust me completely. I can't accept a half-trust: half-trust, or two-thirds trust, won't do for me.' 'But you see there are some extremely delicate matters in those pages.' 'Sir, you are an intelligent and honourable man. You must know that if I begin to read this book and then, at a certain point, am obliged to stop – in effect reach a "no entry" sign – then my imagination will undoubtedly soar far beyond the author's.' 'Yes, of course, you're right: but it is so delicate . . .' 'Forgive me, Rector, but it seems to me it would be best for you to say: Look, here is something which you may not be able to understand very well, so when you have read it I want you to come back and discuss it with me.' 'Very well, excellent! I agree!'

You got everything you wanted.

Yes, but it was because he was a fair-minded man. He was a fair-minded man.

3

THE STAMP OF THE
COUNTER-REFORMATION

*When you entered a seminary you were only four-
teen. That's very young. If a boy of fourteen came to
you today and said he wanted to go into a seminary,
what would you say?*

Before I answer that, I should tell you that in fact when I
entered the seminary I was rather old. Normally in those days
you began at the junior seminary even younger than fourteen. But I lost – or gained – some time. When I started I was
old enough for the fourth class. But I had to go into the third
class because of my Latin.

Had you not done any?

No, not really. My mother was my first teacher, and she
made me work hard. But there came a point when she felt
she couldn't help me any further. She said: 'I've taught you
everything I can. Now I'm going to hand you over to one of
the other teachers. She knows French, which you will need
to know. And she can teach you a lot more history than I
can.'
   I'd like to tell you a story about this second teacher. She
was really a very good teacher; but she relied on certain . . .
stimulants. One of the most important, for her, was the cane.
Wham! It happened on Saturdays. Every Saturday, she
called all the pupils together. Each boy had to ask one of the
other boys a question. If he couldn't answer, or if his answer

was wrong, the boy who had asked the question was invited to answer it himself. And if his answer was correct, he had to cane his ignorant classmate. Wham!

The teacher respected me because I was going to be a priest. One of her brothers had gone into the Church but then he had abandoned the priesthood. In those days, of course, that meant excommunication: the Holy See could not accept it. So she was very fond of me because to her, helping to prepare and shape a future priest was a way of filling the place her brother had abandoned. That was how she looked at things. And I was always set apart from the other boys on Saturdays, at the punishment sessions.

But on one occasion she called to me: 'Helder! Ask a question!' So I asked one of the other boys a question – about something we'd been studying; but he didn't know the answer. The teacher turned to me: 'Well?' I told her the answer. She nodded: 'Now, you know what to do.' But I said: 'I'm sorry, but I can't cane anybody.' 'Then you will be caned yourself!' 'Yes, I should very much prefer that.' 'Class is dismissed! Everybody go home!' To the teacher, my rebellion was outrageous, intolerable.

I thought: 'Now there'll be trouble!' But we went home, and on the way my brother Mardonio – who was only a year older than me, so we were in the same class – said: 'You'll probably be expelled. But I think you were right, all the same. And I don't think Mother and Father will be angry if you tell them the truth.' When we got home I told my parents exactly what had happened. They were entirely sympathetic: they understood immediately. Towards the end of the afternoon the teacher came to see my mother. They shut themselves up in another room for two or three hours. When they came out, the teacher looked sad. After she'd gone, my mother said to me: 'She's going to carry on with her class, and of course she'll take you back. She won't use the cane any more. But at the end of the year she's going to retire. She says she can't teach without the cane.'

So much for my story. But I must answer your question.

In my day there was a junior seminary and a senior seminary. Sometimes boys went to a pre-seminary school first. And sometimes they went to a holiday seminary. In other words, from early childhood until his ordination the future priest was protected, protected, protected. And then one day suddenly he found himself free, without any preparation for liberty or any idea how to deal with it.

It's odd: in those days, when I was in the seminary, we thought it perfectly normal that we should prepare ourselves to serve the people by keeping our distance from them for years and years. Eleven, twelve, thirteen years . . .

Today it isn't like that any more. That's also odd: there are times when you know the Holy Spirit is moving among us. If something changes in a particular place, in a specific town, district or village, you may think it's the result of an idea, or the actions, of an individual or group, or a current fashion. But when it's the same idea and attitude that springs up at more or less the same time, here, there, and everywhere – all over – then you know it's the breath of the Holy Spirit. And that was how it was: suddenly the young men who wanted to be priests felt that the best way of preparing themselves to serve the people was to remain among them. A novice today simply wouldn't dream of going and shutting himself up in an institution for years and years.

> In Écône, in Switzerland, there are some who still prefer to do that.

Yes, I know. But that's the exception that confirms the rule.

In the past, particularly in poorer countries, it was difficult enough for parents to afford to send their children to primary school. Middle school and upper school were even more difficult. So often poor families who wanted their children to get more education would encourage them to go into a seminary. The seminaries would accept the boys even if they said: 'I'm not sure if I have a vocation, but who knows? I am willing, and I *think* I'd like to be a priest.' But in the end what happened was, out of a class of thirty or forty boys only two or three would actually become priests.

> People say that many fewer priests are going into the Church today than in the past. But perhaps they

are comparing the numbers who go into seminaries, as opposed to those who are actually ordained.

It may vary from place to place. As far as Brazil is concerned, I think it's important to point out that the period when most young men wanted to become priests was also a time of extreme clericalism: when everything in the Church had to be done by priests. Of course the laity was necessary as well: lay people had to be there at mass, to say the prayers. And sometimes the clergy asked for their help, in organizing processions or collecting money. They were very good and useful at that. Sometimes certain priests even went so far as to discuss religious matters with the laity and ask their opinions. But final decisions were always taken by the clergy, usually by the bishops.

And since priests had to do everything, decide everything, take every responsibility and since there was no question of the laity sharing their work, or their confidence, it was not surprising that there were so many priests. We needed them. And in order to do anything in the Church, you had to be a priest.

Today it's different. Now the clergy really relies on the laity, and respects its rightful place in the Church of Christ – which is very different from granting it this place as a favour. It's extraordinary how the Church has progressed and evolved. Step by step. Take the Catholic Action movement, for instance: that represented an enormous leap forward. It achieved a great deal; but it was still only a beginning. It merely conceded to the laity the honour of participating in the hierarchical ministry of the Church. The apostle – was the bishop. The apostle's immediate collaborator – was the priest. But certain members of the laity were allowed to participate in the apostolate of the bishops and priests. It was a great honour. There was even some discussion about whether they should be granted the right to 'participate' or to 'collaborate'! It was a very important question! Nowadays we've got beyond all of that. We are very grateful to Catholic Action because it did the pioneering work and blazed the trail. Without it, the Second Vatican Council would probably have been a great deal less effective. But today we really respect the apostolic role of the laity in practice, not just in theory.

> How many members of your class were ordained at the same time as you?

It was an exceptional class: eleven of us went into the senior seminary together, all eleven were ordained, and all eleven of us are still alive and working in the ministry.

> But you aren't all bishops or archbishops?

No . . . the one who was top of the class, Luis Braga, could have been a bishop if he had wished: but he refused. He was like a brother to me. When I went into the seminary he was already there, and I heard that he always won all the prizes, in every subject. So I said to him quite frankly: 'I think I have some good news for you. It must be monotonous for you always to come top like this and never have any competition: so I've decided that I shall do my best to win three of your prizes: for Brazilian literature, Portuguese literature, and French literature. You can keep the rest.' And that was what happened. But we were always very close.

However, you asked me what I would say if a boy of fourteen came and asked me if he might go into a seminary. But the question doesn't arise any more. On the whole there aren't any more boarding seminaries. The pupils live together in small communities. Often they work as well.

> And they are older?

Yes. Usually today you can't enter a seminary until you have finished your secondary education. So you'd be sixteen or seventeen.

These small groups of candidates for the priesthood maintain close contact with a priest, who supervises their progress. And they attend courses at a theological college.

They do more than just philosophy and theology at a theological college these days. In my day, when we graduated from the seminary we were rather proud of ourselves. First of all we had studied the Greek and Latin humanities, and that made us particularly proud. We were convinced that just studying the language and literature of Greece and Rome could develop the mind! Afterwards we did philosophy, and after that, theology. We were utterly convinced that all of this made us rather superior, even compared to other young people of our own age who had studied at the best schools and universities: whether they had studied law, medicine, literature, even philosophy, nothing matched a seminary education!

Imagine our immense surprise, when upon leaving the seminary we encountered young economists, young sociologists, when we found ourselves in a world where science and technology were just beginning to develop. It was a shock, but a providential shock: it made us realize that something had to be changed.

> Which is why today . . .

There was something else as well. We were very ill-prepared for pastoral work, for serving the people. On Sundays we went to give catechism classes to poor children. Normally they were very young children. It was exceptional to have an adolescent in the class. There was no question of our living among the people, or even finding out about real human problems. And so afterwards, we didn't even know how to talk about them. Our language was all wrong. When we preached our sermons were so sophisticated, grounded as they were in Greek and Latin literature, scholastic philosophy and Thomist theology, that they went right over the heads of our congregations.

> You could refute all the heresies of the second or third century, but you couldn't apprehend the realities of the twentieth.

Yes. We bore the stamp of the Counter-Reformation. We in the Church lost a great deal of time because we were so preoccupied with defending ourselves. We were very good at justifying our religion, but it was above all a defensive justification. It's true, we knew how to refute errors. My God! We knew every heresy by heart! We tracked them down, century by century; and we were always on the look out for new ones. In my seminary there was a whole campaign – the Rector wasn't involved – against modernism.

But what I want to emphasize is that when the Spirit of the Lord filled us with the need to come closer to the people we realized that we were strangers to them. All of us. Strangers to the people, especially to the simplest, the humblest, the poorest people. We had to learn their language. And not just their language: their way of thinking, too. We came out of seminary with our heads full of logic. We were Cartesians. We thought in premises and conclusions. We were syllogists, purely and simply. And that isn't how people think. The discovery of reality shocked us all.

> You've often said that you regret not having been taught about social problems in the seminary. But that was the era of Pius XI: his *Quadragesimo anno* appeared the year before you were ordained. And forty years earlier there had been *Rerum novarum*.

When I left the seminary I had only one idea about social matters, and it was quite simple. I had the impression that the world was increasingly divided into two opposing camps: Capitalism and Communism.

> So at least you were taught about Capitalism and Communism in the seminary?

Yes, but in a terribly naive way. Communism was evil, the evil of evils. it was intrinsically perverse.

> Was that in reference to the Russian Revolution, or the works and philosophy of Marx?

Well at that time, you know, people were mainly concerned about Russia. They were afraid of Russia.

> But Russia's a long way from Brazil.

I remember one day a Catholic journalist came to the seminary to give a lecture on social issues. He was a very religious and highly respected man. He wanted to explain to us the symbol of Communism, the hammer and sickle. 'Here is a movement which has chosen for its emblem the hammer and the sickle. The hammer? The symbol of destruction! The sickle? The symbol of death!' Pretty naive, don't you think?

Communism was presented to us above all as bringing death and destruction to religion, and similarly death and destruction to private property. The two things seemed to us equally terrible. For without private property, what would stimulate people to work; and without religion, how could there be morality? What's more, we were told that the Communists preached free love. That was the image we had of Communism.

> And what were you told about Capitalism?

That it was the defender of Christian order.

> Were you told about Father Julio Maria, the Redemptorist who emphasized social questions so prophetically at the turn of the century? A sort of Brazilian Leo XIII.

No, I've no recollection of hearing anything about Father Julio Maria during the whole time I was in the seminary. It was only afterwards that I discovered him, through reading Amoroso Lima. Really, I got a very poor, very naive vision of the world from the seminary; and afterwards I was ready to form the worst opinions. I came out of the seminary with attitudes that shock us today when we meet them in others. But at least that taught me not to condemn people for those attitudes, because I know what it's like, having passed that way myself. Take Dom Jaime de Barros Camara, for example, who was my cardinal at Rio de Janeiro. He was absolutely convinced that Communism was the most terrible, evil thing. He fought against it in every way he could, without doubting for a moment that he was right . . .

It took me some time to discover that a system like Capitalism, which puts profit before people, is also intrinsically evil . . . It is Capitalism which is intrinsically evil.

Even today, when it's no longer possible to talk of Capitalism in the singular, because there are several different forms of it, profit remains the primary concern.

> But during your time in the seminary you must have been subject to some external influences. What did you think of people like Father Leonel Franca, and Jackson de Figueiredo?

It's interesting that you mention two people who were so influential in their own time. Father Franca, of course, had written a book which had made a tremendous impact: *The Church, the Reformation and Civilization*. While I was in the seminary I knew Leonel Franca only through his books. I admired him enormously. When I got to Rio de Janeiro in 1936 I chose him as my spiritual director. I admired him both as a scholar and as a saint.

What is extraordinary is that today when you look at the works of Leonel Franca as a whole it's easy to see that this great mind, this man endowed with a rare, compassionate sensibility, a true saint, was a victim of the apologetic thinking of the Counter-Reformation. His most important book, *The Church, the Reformation and Civilization* is an attack on Protestantism. A Brazilian grammarian, Eduardo Carlos Pirena, had written a book saying that ever since the Reformation the Protestant countries had been in the forefront of progress, while the Catholic countries lagged behind. So Father Leonel Franca summoned all his resources to refute this theory: 'But it isn't true! Catholicism ... etc.' It's easy to see today that his effort was entirely negative.

> What was it that pleased you about Father Leonel Franca's book when you discovered it in the seminary? Did you find it comforting or reassuring – as you did *le Génie du Christianisme*...?

... by Chateaubriand! Yes, perhaps. I know that it delighted us whenever we read it or listened to it ... Of course Leonel Franca also wrote another famous book, against the modernists. He reviewed the articles of a Brazilian philosopher, Oiticica, a fanatical anarchist, criticizing them point by point. And he ended every review with a categorical statement: 'Logical value of this article: nil.' From beginning to end they were 'anti' books: it would be impossible to publish them today.

But at that time they were successful?

Phenomenally so . . .

Did other people in your seminary read them, besides you?

Everybody read them! And not just in the seminaries. Even intelligent people like Alceu Amoroso Lima. Father Leonel Franca really was a great leader, a great innovator. He expounded his theories not only in his books, but also among the groups of disciples who gathered round him. At one point Brazilian teachers and pedagogues discovered the American New School Movement; and immediately Brazilian Catholics, inspired by Father Franca, denounced the 'pragmatism' of the Movement.

They looked for deviation and heresy in everything?

Not only 'pragmatism', but also 'materialism' and even the roots of 'Communism' . . . That was when a Catholic convert, Everardo Backheuser, created the Brazilian Confederation of Catholic Teachers.

You belonged to a small group of seminarists who called themselves 'Jacksonians', disciples of Jackson de Figueiredo. Who was he?

Jackson de Figueiredo was a writer who had the courage to admit he was a Catholic. We admired him enormously for that.

Wasn't he a convert?

Yes he was. But what we found remarkable was that a man of letters, a writer, should have the courage to proclaim himself a Catholic, and use his pen and his talent to fight against errors. He was an exceptional man! But today . . . please don't misunderstand me, I still have as profound a respect for the great Jackson as I have for the memory of Father Leonel Franca, my spiritual director. Jackson de Figueiredo was an outstanding individual. He affected people of every sort: that was his special gift. Rather like a magnetic force that radiated out from within. When I went to Rio de Janeiro I got to know all kinds of people, all very different from one another; and they were all drawn to Jackson. No one could be indifferent to him. Either you hated him and opposed him – and he replied without hesitation: he was a violent, passionate man by nature – or, as in our case, you loved him.

But if you examine his ideas today you can see that, consciously or unconsciously, he was to some extent the inspiration behind Brazilian fascism. Although one mustn't forget that he was vehemently opposed to militarism and dictatorship. He was a man of great complexity: an admirer of Machado de Assis*, Proust and Amiel!

You didn't know him personally?

No. I was still in Fortaleza, reading his books, when I heard the news of his death. Even his death was striking, beautiful. It was on a Sunday. He was swimming in the sea and suddenly he was swept away by a current. Some people on the beach were watching him: they said he struggled for a long time. But when he realized that the current was too strong he made the sign of the cross, folded his arms, and let himself be carried away.

Was he young?

Quite young, I believe. I'm not sure. Thirty-six or thirty-seven at the most.

Would it be true to say that the reason men like Father Leonel Franca and Jackson de Figueiredo

* Joachin Machado de Assis (1839-1908) is generally considered to be Brazil's greatest writer. He wrote *Epitaph for a Small Winner* and *Dom Casmurro*.

made such an impression in the twenties was because
they both preached and expressed the need for a
more 'effective', 'committed' Christianity – which
was after all something quite new in Brazil, where
throughout the nineteenth century at least, the
Gospel had very little to do with life, particularly
with public life?

Yes, it was the novelty of committed, and above all com-
bative, Christianity. That was what aroused and attracted
so many noble, intelligent people. I know that Alceu
Amoroso Lima – like many others – was drawn to Christianity through Jackson. That was the really positive aspect.
It was the passing of a theoretical, individualistic, personal
religion, and the birth of a faith that was involved not just
with Heaven and life after death, but with this world, with
here and now.

Do we know who converted Jackson de Figueiredo,
and where he got his inspiration?

I don't know exactly how he came to be converted. But I do
know that Dom Leme, Cardinal Leme, had a great influence upon him, as he did later upon Amoroso Lima.

It was Dom Leme who published a pastoral letter
in 1916, when he was Archbishop of Recife – before
he became Cardinal at Rio de Janeiro – denouncing
the paradox of Brazilian Catholicism: it was the
religion of the vast majority of the people, yet it was
totally absent from the country's social and political
life.

Yes: 'we are a majority that does nothing, an ineffective
majority.' Dom Leme was another great man of that time.
He certainly prepared the way for Catholic Action. He
founded the Catholic University at Rio de Janeiro. He had
a great influence on the country's intelligentsia: there was a
whole wave of Catholic intellectuals – writers, poets,
musicians – who were inspired by him.
I used the word fascism just now, speaking of Jackson de

Figueiredo. It would be more accurate to say that he was a disciple of Maurras. Fascism came later. He was particularly concerned – perhaps obsessed – with order. It was almost a cult. He founded a journal which he called *A Ordem* – *Order*; it's still going today. And it was no coincidence that he chose Dom Vital as patron of the centre he set up – which is also still in existence. Dom Vital was the Archbishop of Recife who was imprisoned by the Empire in the 1870s because he stirred up the controversy about freemasonry, upholding the prerogatives of spiritual and Christian order against the secular tendencies of the authorities.

I don't want to give the impression that I am deprecating these men: they remain important figures. But I always remember one sentence, one of Jackson de Figueiredo's beliefs, which played a significant part in my life just before and after I was ordained.

I was ordained on 15 August 1931. The year before that, in 1930, what was referred to as 'the Brazilian revolution' had begun in São Paulo. I was absolutely opposed to this revolution, which finally brought Vargas to power. I was against it because Jackson de Figueiredo had taught me that 'the best revolution is worse than the worst legality'. You understand? For me that became a fact, a profound conviction. 'The best revolution is worse than the worst legality.' Well! You can imagine how attached I was to authority and the social order.

> But when Jackson de Figueiredo spoke of order, did he not mean it in the philosophical and theological sense? Because it seems to me that he was not very satisfied with the social order, for example. He was even rather opposed to Capitalism, wasn't he?

Yes, that's true. But if you say that any kind of legality is always better than the best revolution, don't you understand that it means that you are opposed to change? So that even if, in theory, you condemn Capitalism, in practice the anti-revolutionary conviction is stronger.

It's true that we have never experienced a true revolution

in Brazil. The so-called Brazilian revolutions have brought about only very minor changes. When Brazil left the Portuguese Empire to set up its own independent Empire, it was the son of the King of Portugal who became Emperor of Brazil. It was more of a continuation than a change. And later, when we went from Empire to Republic, and from one Republic to another, each time it was one élite group taking the place of another élite group. It is always the privileged who, by one means or another, keep themselves in power. They never look to the people, who have nothing to do with these 'revolutions'.

4
THE THIRTIES:
THE TURNING-POINT

> You were fortunate in leaving the seminary and entering the world, so to speak, at a time that was particularly interesting and important in the history of Brazil. Even if there weren't any 'revolutions', there were plenty of disturbances.

People often say that the years just before and just after 1930 were decisive for Brazil: that they were marked by a threefold revolution – political, cultural and religious.

The major political development of that time was 'the lieutenants' movement'.

The country was dominated by the privileged classes: they had absolute power. But the two richest states, São Paulo and Minas Gerais, shared the monopoly of this power.

You can understand how the young soldiers felt. The lieutenants wanted to shake up these oligarchies a bit: they were looking for ways of reforming the system. These young lieutenants were quite sincere. You have to understand that here in Brazil the trained army staff, who are closer to the soldiers than their officers, often come from the working classes, from the very poorest families. We do have conscription, compulsory military service. But it wasn't very difficult for the children of wealthy parents to avoid it. The working-class people couldn't do that. So these young men from the interior came to the cities, to Rio de Janeiro, the capital, and discovered a whole new world. They saw and heard things that they had never seen or heard before. They had access to clothes, food, and pleasures such as they had never dreamed of. Very often they were disorientated.

The lieutenants tended to come from the middle classes, from the lower middle classes.

At that time we were still practising slavery in Brazil. But the great wind of liberation was beginning to blow, largely thanks to philosophers like Joaquim Nabuco and poets like Castro Alves: and the slave masters, as they were called, asked the army for protection. The army replied that it was not an army of slave hunters. So the *grands seigneurs* had to set up their own militia – the National Guard – to guard or recover their slaves. The people they chose as colonels of the National Guard were prepared to go hunting for runaway slaves. When slaves were caught and brought back they were brutally punished. The army would have nothing to do with it.

While I was in the seminary, persuaded by Jackson de Figueiredo that 'the best revolution is worse than the worst legality', I couldn't understand or approve of these young lieutenants who wanted things to change. But today I see their aspirations as refreshing and quite reasonable: they wanted to put an end to the monopoly of São Paulo and Minas Gerais.

The *café au lait* republic . . .

Yes: São Paulo, the capital of coffee, and Minas Gerais, rich from cattle farming . . . The lieutenants demanded that voting in elections be done by secret ballot, for example. Because elections were really scandalous – a mockery.

Did everyone have the right to vote?

No, not everyone. But at least we had elections. And in the interior they were rigged. In the towns, which were just beginning to expand, the opposition had a slight chance of winning: there was some sense of public conscience. But in the interior, in the countryside, we were living – still are living – in the Middle Ages, with lords and masters, and barons and baronesses.

On the great plantations there is always a *casa grande* – the master's house – and the *senzala*. The *senzala* is where the slaves live.

Once I decided to visit a plantation to see for myself what it was like. It was an *engenho de açucar* – a sugar plantation. I went there for the feast of the patron saint of this plantation, the *Padroeiro*, as we call it. I wanted to live exactly like the priests who are attached to these 'parishes'. At about six o'clock in the evening everyone assembled around the landowner and his family. I was there as the landowner's guest: and I had to speak to all these workers, who were forbidden to move or make a noise. After I'd finished speaking I invited them all to midnight mass. It wasn't Christmas, but it was the feast of the *Padroeiro*. Then I went to the *casa grande* to share a lavish meal with the landowner, the *grand seigneur*, while the workers went back to their poor houses where they lived in sub-human conditions...

When was this?

After I came to Recife, in 1964 or 1965. I wanted to experience it for myself, to give myself a jolt. After dinner I said to the *seigneur*: 'Forgive me. I have absolutely no desire to hurt you. I know that you are not the only one to blame, nor the most guilty. We in the Church failed to open the eyes of your grandparents and your parents, perhaps we are the most responsible... I will not sleep here, in the *casa grande*; I will go to the *senzala*. I prefer to stay with a poor family.'

The landowner was flabbergasted. He couldn't believe it. But he made a suggestion: 'Since you say that we are not the only ones to blame, won't you do me the favour of sleeping in the chapel instead?' I agreed, and spent the night in the chapel. But really, even in the chapel, I was still the guest of the landowner, because it belonged to his estate. It was there so that the good words of religion would help the workers to accept, to resign themselves. The opium of the people...

Could we get back to the lieutenants in 1930?...

The lieutenants knew that the landowners, the slave masters, the employers in the interior disposed of their workers' votes as they pleased. It was impossible for a worker, a poor man, to vote differently from his master. The lieutenants hoped that if elections were held in secret people would have more chance of expressing themselves and coming to power. But their revolution didn't have that effect. The most obvious effect was that the state of Rio Grande do Sul seized the opportunity of challenging the power of São Paulo and Minas Gerais. It was the same old story. The lieutenants had really acted positively with good intentions: but their efforts didn't bring about a structural change, only a change of boss – or rather a change among the bosses. They were still playing the same game. And the country was still run on a system of internal colonialism. The *seigneurs* were still in power. For the people, nothing had changed.

> Was it this revolution of 1930 that triggered off Carlos Prestes' 'long march'?

No: that was earlier. Carlos Prestes was one of the lieutenants involved in the 1924 revolt. But he wasn't satisfied with the outcome: he wanted to go further, to achieve structural reform. Instead of going back to his barracks he set off with a little group of revolutionaries to march across the countryside, going from village to village. He wanted to make contact with the people, to wake them up. He had to keep moving all the time because there were government agents pursuing him. People called it 'the Prestes column'. The march lasted from 1924 to 1926.

> Was Prestes a Communist? The Communist Party had been formed in 1922 . . .

He wasn't at the beginning, but he became a Communist in 1930. In fact he became the great hero, the great myth of the Brazilian Communist Party. He's living in exile now, but he's still the president of the party. At least, of the 'orthodox' branch of the party; there are other branches that claim to be more revolutionary – Trotskyists and Maoists. But to the classical Communists, Prestes is still their great leader.

> Were there many people in his column?

No, it was just a small group. But he caught the imagination of a great number of people. Eventually, of course, Prestes was thrown out of the army. Then in 1935 the Communist Party was outlawed by Getúlio Vargas. Prestes was put in prison.

So you see the political 'revolution' began with noble ideas, but it didn't change very much.

At the same time there was a cultural revolution, which was begun by a group of young writers and artists who organized a festival of modern art in 1922. What these young people wanted was a literature that was less remote and alienated, that had more to do with the people, was closer to reality – while remaining, of course, in communion with the universal, with humanity as a whole. They wanted to give expression to the most unique, most characteristic aspects of our mentality, our way of thinking. They even wanted to alter the language. As you know we speak Portuguese: but over the centuries our pronunciation and accent have changed, and in some cases even our vocabulary and the meaning of words. These young writers wanted Brazilian literature to be written in the language that was spoken in Brazil, rather than the language that was spoken in Portugal, as it had always been before.

I sometimes think this cultural movement had more effect than the political one. It really marked a break with the past. I've already mentioned José de Alencar and his romantic presentation of the Indians; it was beautiful, and moving, particularly to us North-Easterners in Ceará. But it was nevertheless an alienated, remote literature: it wasn't an expression of the people, of the Indians, but of a trans-figured idea of the people. And the language was very, very classical.

But after 1920 things changed. The 'modernists', as they were called, overthrew the old ideas and manners. Some people called them sacrilegious. But they didn't just destroy things, or make fun, or publish pamphlets: they wrote poems and novels on new themes, typically Brazilian, and in a new Brazilian language. It really was the start of a new literature.

It was a movement from romanticism to realism, at the same time as surrealism was developing in Europe...

Yes, if you like. It wouldn't be true to say that this new Brazilian literature was politically committed, or revolutionary. But it was concerned with reality. People wrote, for instance, about the cultivation of sugar cane. Several writers described the condition of the sugar cane workers. Others wrote about coffee workers, or about sailors, or fishermen, and so on. It seems to me this literary revolution did more for the Brazilian people than the political revolution.

And the religious revolution?

Yes, you could say there was a religious revolution as well. It bore no comparison with what happened later, at the Second Vatican Council, or at Medellín. But all the same, it was the beginning of the beginning. At first we had only the general Catholic Action, with four branches: men, women, boys and girls. It was merely a question of the laity 'collaborating with the hierarchy'. But at least it was an invitation, a way of acknowledging the laity, making room for it. And Catholic Action began to look at things in the light of the Gospel, which helped enormously to make people more aware. Later Catholic Action became specialized, with branches for different sectors of the community: factory workers, people of independent means, farm workers, university people . . .

I think perhaps you're going a little too fast there: Catholic Action only became specialized – in Brazil and elsewhere – in the forties and fifties...

I'm sorry, but you know I've never been very good on dates. However, it's still true to say that Catholic Action prepared the way.

There's one person who stands at the crossroads of the threefold revolution: political, cultural and religious: your friend Alceu Amoroso Lima, who today, at over eighty years old, is still one of the major figures in contemporary Brazil.

In my opinion, Amoroso Lima is the greatest living Brazilian. He is a convert to the Roman Catholic faith. Before his conversion he thought and lived like a dilettante, an enlightened amateur, an epicurean, as he often says himself. He was, and is, a fine scholar and a distinguished critic. I remember a book he devoted to one of our authors: he worked on it for seven years, like a sculptor creating a statue, with love and passion. But after his conversion he felt the need to work for the cause of Christianity, to spread ideas, to help all kinds of people ask themselves questions and find the answers. He wrote, for instance, for jurists, asserting that a jurist who claims to be a Christian must conform to certain criteria. He did the same for biologists, politicians . . .

He is a true Christian, a man of God, but he has remained a man of letters, a man of great artistic sensibility. It was he more than anyone else who helped Brazil to understand modernism. He was the great critic of modernism . . .

By 'modernism' you mean 'modern art'?

Yes, the rebirth of Brazilian literature, the cultural liberation with regard to Portugal, Brazil's desire to be itself, while retaining links and contact with the rest of the world. It's clear that if it hadn't been for Amoroso Lima the young writers who ventured along this path would never have been understood. Amoroso Lima interpreted them. I even think that he sometimes helped them to understand themselves. Because you know a writer – particularly a poet – is not capable of analysing his own work. He lives, he perceives, he creates. When he sees how someone like Amoroso Lima interprets his work, he may be astonished: 'To think that all that was inside me and I didn't know!' It's the same with musicians or painters.

Amoroso Lima was also the great interpreter of our modern architecture, painting and music – of Villa-Lobos and Portinari. We have some fine artists in Brazil: they would be acclaimed even in 'advanced' countries.

And it's true that Amoroso Lima also interpreted the political revolution. Although he had been so strongly influenced by Jackson de Figueiredo he had an extraordinary breadth of vision. He could see what was positive about 'the lieutenants' movement'. He realized that even if it wasn't a revolution in the true sense of the word – a profound structural change, a radical shift – nevertheless it was a step forward, it had had some effect. And of course he was also the leader of the religious revolution.

Did he remain leader for a long time?

Yes, because Cardinal Leme always trusted him completely, absolutely. But Cardinal Leme's successor, Jaime de Barros Camara, didn't feel the same way: he was always rather suspicious of Amoroso Lima because of Maritainism*.

Because Amoroso Lima had first introduced – and again interpreted – the works of Jacques Maritain in Brazil and in the rest of Latin America?

Yes, the first Maritain, who wrote *Integral Humanism**. Certain people detected in his works and philosophy a distinct smell of heresy . . . Goodness knows how many times I and my brother-priest and later brother-bishop, José Vincente Távora, went to Cardinal Camara to try to make him understand Amoroso Lima...The cardinal didn't suspect him personally, nor his intentions. But he always had a priest with him who examined every sentence and word, and found fault with something or other.

It was like that in those days. I remember once when I was in Rome, at the State Secretariat, talking to a man called Giovanni Battista Montini. After a very friendly, fraternal conversation, he produced a copy of a publication which had appeared in Brazil, in my diocese of Rio de Janeiro. It was a journal published by a group of young Catholic women, which had found its way to Rome, where it had been examined: and now it was in the desk of the Pro-Secretary of State at the Vatican, all underlined in red ink as if it were

* Jacques Maritain (1882-), French philosopher.
Integral Humanism (1974) University of Notre Dame Press.

some important theological treatise. Someone had gone through it picking out any possible heresies, and marked them all in red ink!

So I smiled, and the future Pope Paul VI smiled back, because he understood exactly: 'Excellency, it is a great joy to know that you are here, and to be able to rely on your understanding and breadth of vision! Because with all this suspicion that is rife, all this examining of texts, I begin to wonder if even the pastoral letters of our bishops are safe from the red pen. And I'm quite sure that certain passages in the Gospel could be censored. For instance, the Magnificat is a revolutionary hymn: it's disturbing, it's serious, it's agitation! It speaks out against the established order, against the rich and powerful! It may not be Communism, but it prepares the way for Communism. No doubt someone will underline it in red ink! So it is a great joy, Excellency, to know that you are here.' Monsignor Montini smiled ...

Amoroso Lima knew what it was like, as a Christian, to be suspected by his own Church. It caused him a great deal of suffering. But it seemed to make him greater. To everyone who knows him, including me, he gives the impression of growing younger every day. He is a man of iron: of really remarkable moral strength. He is the only man in Brazil today who can speak the truth in the *Jornal do Brasil,* and the censor dare not interfere with his words. The only possible explanation is that this absolute moral strength commands respect on all sides. And also, no doubt, while he has always vehemently denounced and attacked injustice, oppression and falsehood, Amoroso Lima has always avoided offending individuals.

Another product of the twenties was Getúlio Vargas. His career began with the 1930 revolution and lasted until 1945 – even longer, in fact. Who was Vargas?

Vargas ... was a strange, very complex man. He came from Rio Grande do Sul, a state that was run by internal colonialism, with huge *fazendas* and masses of *peones* – farm-labourers. He managed to become a dictator whom the people really loved.

But he wasn't a dictator to begin with...

No. The 1930 revolution took him to Rio de Janeiro. Then in 1934 he got a new constitution passed and he was elected president. In 1937 after a *coup d'état* he founded the *Estado Novo*, and gave himself absolute power, which he kept until 1945.

A journalist once said to Vargas: 'Mister President, do you think you have any enemies?' Vargas thought for a moment, walked up and down the room, and then gave an answer which may appear cynical, but really expresses his way of conducting politics: 'I can't think of any enemy that I couldn't turn into a good friend in twenty-four hours.' In other words, he understood human weakness entirely, and he knew how to manipulate people. He knew some men could be won with flattery, some with honours, some with money. And as far as the people were concerned, he presented himself as a friendly dictator.

'Friendly' and 'dictator' are two words that don't usually go together...

Vargas gave the Brazilian people their first employment legislation – like a present. It included every conceivable protection for the workers, for women, children and old people. He legalized and organized trade unions. The people were overjoyed.

Vargas also founded the Brazilian Labour Party. It was a wonderful way of exploiting the workers' approval of the new social measures. But since these measures had been devised and passed without any participation from the people, bestowed on them like a gift instead of fought for and won, the workers simply weren't ready to receive them or use them properly. You can't compare Vargas' Labour Party with the British Labour Party, for instance. Vargas was essentially concerned with winning popular support through a policy that the people had nothing to do with.

Some years later the heir to Vargas' political ideas, João Goulart, was persuaded that he could rely on the workers, specifically on the General Labour Confederation, for support against right-wing forces. That was in 1964. But this confederation existed only in his head, and on paper, because we haven't really got a trade union tradition in Brazil: the unions were created from above, by a popular dictator. Right from the beginning, since neither Vargas nor his successors liked the idea of having a union official elected by his fellow workers, the Minister of Labour has always appointed another official, the *pelego*. We have no union tradition: but we have a tradition of 'peleguism'. The 'revolution' of 1964 gave the Minister of Labour the opportunity of legally replacing every union official considered unreliable.

> Could one compare Vargas' 'friendly' dictatorship with that of Perón in Argentina?

People have often made that comparison, because Vargas and Perón were both very popular in their own countries. I remember the time when I was immersed in the *favelas* of Rio de Janeiro. I got to know them very well. I used to say that the three things that had most influence in every *mocambo*, every hovel, were Saint George, Flamengo and Vargas...

> Not Carlos Prestes?

No. Because you see the Brazilian people are still a long way even from socialism, yet alone Communism.

> Flamengo is a Rio de Janeiro football club. But why Saint George, and not Our Lady of Aparecida?

Our Lady of Aparecida is well-known and well-loved throughout the country, but particularly in the neighbourhood of the shrine, near São Paulo. In Rio it is Saint George that the people venerate.

So you see: Saint George, Flamengo, Vargas.

Vargas was forced to resign in 1945. And then he came back for a short time in 1951, as an elected president. His downfall was tragic. There was a journalist who was beginning to specialize in bringing down governments...

Carlos Lacerda?

Carlos Lacerda. He began his campaign by criticizing what he called the 'quagmire' surrounding the president. Vargas had a personal guard, and in this guard was a certain Gregorio, a Negro. Lacerda accused Gregorio of corruption and making 'shady deals'. He never attacked Vargas personally and directly, always his entourage. The scandal reached such a pitch that Vargas was forced to dismiss his personal guard. Carlos Lacerda was protected by the military, who were already preparing to take over from Vargas. One day an airforce lieutenant who was involved with Lacerda was assassinated. But the assassin had obviously intended to kill Lacerda himself. This caused such a tremendous upsurge of feeling that the people who had been following Lacerda's campaign in the newspapers were ready to riot in the streets.

The Cardinal of Rio de Janeiro felt obliged to attend the funeral of the lieutenant who had been killed. So we were all there, the cardinal and all his bishops, in the great church. As we came out I said to Dom Jaime: 'Your Eminence, I want to make a suggestion.' And he said: 'I think I can guess what it is, and I agree. In order to show that we are not committed to either camp, that we are not politicians, we should go and visit President Vargas. Will you ask for an audience?'

That was exactly what I was going to suggest. I realized that Vargas had his back to the wall, and I feared that he might try and commit suicide.

The presidential palace was deserted, and the cardinal and I were invited to go and see Vargas at once. He was wearing dark glasses, which was unusual for him. Obviously he had been weeping. He received us in a small library in one corner of the abandoned palace. For the first time in my life I understood what writers mean when they talk about 'rats leaving the sinking ship'. All his false friends had deserted him in his hour of trouble, as false friends always do. The palace was empty.

The cardinal simply said: 'Mister President, I felt I should pay you a visit.' And Vargas, who was normally so taciturn, even with his close friends, talked solidly for half an hour. It was obvious that he felt the need to talk. He said: 'Your Eminence, I thank you with all my heart . . . Thank you. I am not a man of hatred . . .' And he talked, and talked.

As we came out of the palace I said to the cardinal: 'Vargas is close to death. I'm afraid he will commit suicide.' And indeed he did.

And immediately we had another lesson in popular psychology. The middle classes and the rich were just getting ready to celebrate Vargas' downfall. But as soon as the news of the president's suicide broke and his last message had been broadcast on the radio, the people – the workers, the poor people – took to the streets to find Carlos Lacerda and lynch him. Monsignor Távora managed to forestall them: he warned Lacerda and gave him a chance to escape. But this didn't stop Lacerda, several years later on the eve of the military 'revolution' of 1964, denouncing Dom Távora's movement for basic education as 'subversive' . . . That's human weakness . . .

5

A KIND OF FASCISM
CALLED INTEGRALISM

I think Carlos Lacerda will come up again during
the course of our interviews. But for the moment I
should like you to bring to life another man whom
you were close to, and who was also influential in
the thirties: Plínio Salgado, founder of Integralismo,
the Brazilian fascist movement.

Yes, Plínio Salgado...He's dead now, but I knew him well. He
was a man of letters, a writer. He wrote novels. And then he
became a philosopher. He wanted to be a political leader as
well, the leader of leaders, but that was a mistake: he wasn't
cut out for it.

In 1933 Plínio Salgado published the Integralist Manifesto.
It was more or less a Brazilian version of the fascism of
Mussolini, or Hitler, above all it was similar to the corpor-
atism of Salazar.

Integralist Action involved wearing a green shirt and
swearing an oath of loyalty to the national leader, a gran-
diose vision of the country in which all the regions would be
united and distances reduced, a philosophy which claimed to
be integral and spiritualist, a preoccupation with Communism and a determination to oppose it, and a slogan: God,
Country and Family ...

For a time I was deeply involved with the Integralist
movement. I think many other young people at that time
had a similar experience – and not just in Brazil. When I said

my first mass in 1931 – at the age of twenty-two, with a special dispensation from the Pope – the assistants who knelt beside me were two young lieutenants, Severino Sombra and Jeova Mota. Sombra had been introduced to me by Amoroso Lima. I wrote to Amoroso Lima to express my sorrow at the death of Jackson de Figueiredo, and to hail him as the new leader of Brazilian Catholicism. In his reply he said: 'A young lieutenant will come to visit you in Fortaleza. He is a convert; I am sure that you will like one another, and that you will work together.'

Severino Sombra was steeped in the corporatist ideas of Salazar. He was also inclined to sympathize with Hitler, and even more with Mussolini. He really admired Mussolini. As soon as he came to Fortaleza we set up a Labour Legion. Sombra came to the meetings not in his army uniform but in a Mussolini-style shirt.

When Plínio Salgado began to think about forming Integralist Action he wrote to various people who were already engaged in similar sorts of work all over Brazil. He wrote to Severino Sombra, asking him to be the leader of Integralist Action in Ceará. He asked me to be secretary for education in Ceará. I asked my archbishop if I should accept, and he told me I should. Integralism was still not clearly defined, and Dom Manuel da Silva Gomes sensed instinctively that the movement would have a great attraction for young people and the workers.

Plínio Salgado was primarily an intellectual, a writer and an orator. He was very short and very thin. Like a mouse, or a little rat. But when he spoke he was transfigured.

In my opinion the masses were so hungry and thirsty for a word of hope and love, that the doctrine of Integralism seemed to answer their needs. This was particularly true of us young people, who felt these needs most urgently, it was like bread, like food: so a whole intellectual élite was captivated by Plínio Salgado's ideas.

While I was secretary for education in the Cearan branch of Integralist Action, I was summoned to Rio de Janeiro to take part in a Roman Catholic conference on education. I remember that I was accorded special privileges as an official of Integralist Action. But I used to get away from the conference as often as I could to go and attend Integralist meetings, with Plínio. I met some of the most brilliant, lively young people of Rio there, including, for instance, Santiago Dantas. I still consider him one of the most brilliant men I have ever met. A genius, if you like. He was gifted with an intense perception of people and things. I still remember the first time I met him, and our first conversation: he talked about the end of the century, about the year 2000, just as if he had already experienced it.

It was a strange generation. Like Amoroso Lima, Santiago Dantas was by temperament something of an epicurean, a dilettante. He was devoted to the arts and loved beautiful things. But at the same time, by education and by conviction, he was dedicated to the people and to the cause of human advancement. In a sense he had already gone beyond Integralism. He'd had the idea of taking over a newspaper – the old *Jornal do comercio* – and transforming it; but unfortunately he didn't manage to assemble a good enough editorial team to do what others later did with the *Jornal do Brasil* . . .

We became very close friends, Santiago Dantas and I. We were both members of the Supreme Council of Integralist Action. But I wanted to tell you a story about that.

When I left Fortaleza and went to Rio de Janeiro, in January 1936, the Archbishop of Rio, Cardinal Leme, received me warmly. He asked me to give up Integralism, which I did willingly as I was beginning to see things very differently.

One day Plínio Salgado summoned me for a private interview. He confessed that he was worried. He was convinced that Integralism would eventually come to power: but he was overwhelmed by the enormous responsibility that faced him, particularly because of the oath of loyalty that every member of the movement had taken on his name. He had formed a Chamber of Forty to share this responsibility, but it was too large to be efficient. He had decided to form a Supreme Council with only twelve members, and he wanted me to be one of them. He knew that my answer had come from the cardinal, so now he asked me to explain the new project and his proposal to Dom Leme.

After the Integralist March – the Brazilian equivalent of Mussolini's March on Rome – in which Getúlio Vargas took part from his palace at Catete, Dom Leme became firmly convinced that Integralism would soon come to power. He told me to accept Plínio's offer, but on two conditions: the meetings of the Supreme Council must always take place on neutral ground; and my name must not appear in public among those of council members. I would be a kind of padre to the movement. In fact the Integralist newspaper often referred to me as both a priest and a member of the council.

Then Plínio called me to another secret meeting. Vargas had just sent his Minister of Justice, Francisco de Campos, to him, with the message that he intended to present the country with a new constitution, dissolve parliament and proclaim the *Estado Novo*. It was five days before the *coup d'état*.

Plínio felt obliged to provide the cardinal with a copy of the text of the new constitution, and he asked me to carry out this mission.

The cardinal thanked Plinio for his consideration, read the new constitution and noted its terms. But it was understood that he would not officially admit to knowing about this totalitarian charter, to avoid giving the impression of connivance.

Plínio cherished the illusion that he would be called on to be the Prime Minister, the true *Führer*. At that time in many places there were more Integralists than policemen. But Vargas recognized Plínio Salgado's weakness and a few days after the proclamation of the *Estado Novo*, he outlawed Integralism. There was really very little reaction to the ban and Plínio was exiled.

But to come back to Santiago Dantas.

After Vargas had outlawed the party in 1937, Dantas held a luncheon for all the most valuable young Integralists of the time. He was good enough to invite me. I remember exactly what he said to us: 'Friends, all of us here have a public vocation. So let us not lose touch with one another: remain alert, and available. Let us not be defeated by this first setback in our political and public lives. On the contrary, we should profit from the experience. The lesson it has taught us is clear and easy to understand: it should open our eyes and help us in the future. So let us not lose touch.'

We remained, he and I, very close to one another, very good friends. One day he said to me: 'I have decided to join Getúlio Vargas Labour Party. I have no illusions about it. I shall never be influential in the party, because the middle classes will never forgive me for having abandoned them, and the workers will never be able to trust me. But nevertheless I think I can be useful, so it is a sacrifice I am happy to make.'

> And what happened to him? Was he able to be useful?

Yes, yes, he became Minister of Finance...

> Under Vargas?

No, later. Under João Goulart, I think. But you know, when it comes to dates . . . He was also Minister for Foreign Affairs: in fact he initiated a cultural revolution in the Foreign Affairs Ministry by bringing together a group of bright young people and organizing a course of study to prepare them for diplomatic work. Normally Brazilian ambassadors were career diplomats who were very remote from the realities of the country. Sometimes politicians or military men were awarded ambassadorships as an honour. But Santiago felt that diplomats should really know about the major social problems. So he created this totally new atmosphere of work and study.

One day, when I heard that he was ill – he had cancer – I went to visit him at his house. While I was there he left the room for a moment to get a book. He read a great deal, and had an impressive library. He was like a walking library himself. I knew that he was no longer practising the faith. But while he was out of the room I noticed on a table exactly twelve figures of Christ in the form of the Crucifixion, but without the cross. I was looking at them when he came back, and he said: 'My friend, not long from now you will see me in that condition.' And it was true: I saw him, at his house, at the height of his suffering. He came face to face with Christ, and he asked to receive communion.

Another memory I have of Santiago Dantas: when parliamentary government was introduced in Brazil, Dantas was one of the candidates proposed for the premiership. The campaign was a real struggle, orchestrated by the press and radio and television. Santiago was up all night following the voting. And he was defeated. But when the television reporters came to interview him afterwards he was a model of moral superiority and wisdom. Instead of dwelling on his defeat and disappointment, he said: 'We should not be concerned with the question of individuals: we must look at the country's problems, the real social problems.'

> I'd like to come back to the Labour Legion that you set up in the year you were ordained, 1931, with the lieutenants Severino Sombra and Jeova Mota. What was its aim?

The *Legião Cearense do Trabalho* was a movement along the lines of Salazar's corporatism. We recruited a vast number of people: practically the entire working population of Fortaleza, and a number of small groups in the Cearan interior. We were even strong enough to call and organize strikes. Our aim was to defend workers who were being exploited – through inadequate salaries, or intolerable working conditions.

Once for instance, we organized a strike at Light, a Canadian company that controlled the distribution of electricity in Fortaleza. We investigated the situation thoroughly and found that every possibility of negotiating with the management had been exhausted. We began by calling a strike in the distribution centre. We said that if the management didn't accept the workers' claims within forty-eight hours we would extend the strike to the public electricity supply, and plunge Fortaleza into darkness. We were convinced that would bring us victory.

But it didn't work. The distribution workers did go on strike, but we didn't use our 'big guns' after all. We thought about it a great deal, and finally we decided that we didn't have the right to deprive the whole town of light and power. We didn't want to be responsible for all the stupid things that might happen – and the crimes that might be committed – because of the disruption.

We organized other strikes, but the results were always questionable. These experiences left me with the conviction that strikes are a very difficult and dangerous weapon. We always set out enthusiastically with everyone in agreement and feeling cheerful. But we must have looked really pathetic to the employers. They knew we weren't strong enough either to hold out or to carry out our threats. We used to ask the public to support the strikers, but you see the people who could really have helped us – the middle classes – were naturally opposed to the strikes. Gradually the strikers' enthusiasm waned, and the strike had to be called off. No, I came to the conclusion that strikes are a weapon that is very very difficult to handle. Perhaps the secret of successful industrial action is the combination of strike and boycott, as practised by Cesar Chavez and his followers in Delano, in the United States.

It was at that time, too, that I started to write: in the Labour Legion's newspaper, *Bandeirantes*, which only appeared twice, and in Fortaleza's Catholic daily newspaper, *O Nordeste*. We used the collective pseudonym Agathon. On one occasion I had the audacity to sign myself Athanase. Later I adopted the pen name Alceu da Silveira, in honour of both my mentor Alceu Amoroso Lima and the great Catholic poet Tasso da Silveira, whose work I admired enormously. The articles I wrote were fairly flimsy, and extremely right-wing.

Meanwhile, in São Paulo, Plínio Salgado was setting out the ideological principles of Integralism in his journal *A Razao*.

You were saying earlier that he had most influence with the intellectual élite.

Yes, an intellectual élite was drawn to Integralism, but Plínio Salgado and his ideas attracted vast numbers of ordinary people as well, not only in the cities like Rio de Janeiro and São Paulo, but also in small towns. Vast numbers of men and vast numbers of women – because there

was a women's branch of Integralism as well. It's extraordinary, but even very simple, poor people put on the green
shirt.

Integralist Action wasn't a party. Plínio Salgado didn't
like the word party: it conjured up 'part', 'apart', 'departure', 'fraction'. He wanted to be a whole, to represent
the whole. He chose the Greek letter *sigma* as the symbol of
the movement. And it's true, he brought together a body of
people that included workers, the young, and the whole
intellectual élite.

> Was it his ideas, his doctrine, or his eloquence that
> attracted them?

We all knew quite well that Plínio Salgado was not, and
couldn't be, the leader he claimed to be. But he exercised a
kind of magic power that raised and galvanized our hopes.
Of course you could say that he sometimes behaved and
spoke like a demagogue. But demagogy is difficult to define
and recognize. If a demagogue is someone who understands
how the people's minds work, who can speak in words and
signs that the people understand, and is concerned not with
himself but with the good of the people – then I'm not afraid
of a demagogue! Think of the passage in the Gospel where
the crowd shouts to Jesus: 'Behold, thy mother and thy
brethren stand without . . .' And Jesus looks at the crowd and
says: 'Whosoever shall do the will of my Father which is in
Heaven, the same is my brother, and sister, and mother.'
Obviously the crowd understood him instantly: no doubt
they applauded. But that doesn't mean to say that Christ
was a demagogue . . .

What Plínio Salgado lacked was the ability to make a
decision. Once when we were at Santiago Dantas' house
Francisco de Compos told us, in a semi-monologue that was
very typical of him: 'When I brought Plínio the message
from Vargas about the *coup d'état* and the *Estado Novo* – if
Plínio had reacted, if he'd thrown me out of the house, I'd
have joined the movement. But his lack of response, his
passivity, his weakness proved to me beyond doubt that the
myth of the national leader was totally unfounded.'

While he was in exile in Portugal he wrote a book about Christ. It was an evangelical discourse, but with a strong dose of ideology, Integralist ideology. It was his vision of the Gospel . . .

When he came back from Portugal Plinio Salgado unfortunately decided to found a political party that was just like any other political party. Of course I wouldn't have wanted him to try to revive Integralism: but I'd have preferred him to accept the lesson of his political defeat and return to writing novels – or even philosophy. But instead he had this awful idea of forming a political party of the worst sort, a small party that made every conceivable alliance . . .

> Rather like the MRP* in France, except in size – the MRP wasn't a small party.

Yes, that's right.

> And it was at the same time, too: in 1945, after the fall of Vargas, at the end of the Second World War.

Yes, it was the same time. It's really curious to see these mysterious links between events in one country and another: a communication that takes place between the people involved even without them knowing it, as if the course of history were directed by something in the air at the time that pays no attention to frontiers, rather than by the people who claim to be responsible . . .

> All in all, did anything survive from Integralism? Was there any link between the Integralism of the thirties and the Integrism of the fifties and sixties?

I think the legacy of Integralism is very sad. Its positive aspects – the emphasis on understanding the people and being understood by them, making them more aware, speaking of God and of deeper values, all of that disappeared. In a sense the 1964 *coup d'état* was a victory for all the negative aspects of Integralism. You have to remember that Integralism was widespread in the armed forces, particularly the navy. It was hard to find a lieutenant, or an admiral, who

* Mouvement Républican Populaire

wasn't an Integralist. Some of them were convinced anti-Communists. But for others that was just a pretext, a slogan, a convenient flag. It must be obvious to everyone today that the Capitalist and Communist Super Powers – say the United States and the USSR – are only too happy to exploit their differences and co-exist peacefully when it suits them. I remember I once said to my cardinal at Rio de Janeiro: 'The real problem is not the confrontation between East and West, it's the confrontation between North and South!'

> Integralism was inspired by the theories of Salazar. Mussolini also had his followers on this side of the Atlantic. But what about Franco? Did the Spanish Civil War have any repercussions in Brazil? Did it affect people's attitudes to fascism?

In some small groups, yes, certainly. Bernanos came to Brazil at that time, visiting Minas and Rio. The groups of followers that formed around him were vividly aware of the war in Spain, and of what it really represented: a rehearsal and a preparation for the Second World War. But you see generally, to people who were obsessed by Communism, in other words to the entire Christian community – bishops, priests and laity, apart from a few exceptions, and I wasn't one of them – the war in Spain represented a massacre of martyrs by Communists. We were absolutely convinced that Communism was the enemy of Christ's Church: it murdered priests, threw nuns out of convents, burned churches, committed all kinds of atrocities. So Franco was really the defender of Christian civilization, you see?

My God! I really sympathize with Augustine, Saint Augustine, who fell prey to a new delusion every time he escaped from an old one! No sooner had I torn myself away from Integralism than I joined the Catholic Electoral League, in the belief that Brazil enjoyed the best system of relations between Church and State!

6

FROM ONE DELUSION
TO ANOTHER

Let us go back a bit: the Catholic Electoral League was formed by Cardinal Leme at the time of the elections to the Constituent Assembly in 1934?

The cardinal didn't want a Catholic party. His idea was to present a programme to candidates of every party and give them an assurance that if they committed themselves to this programme they would receive the support of Catholic voters. 'Here is a list of the principles we adhere to. Look at it. If you agree to respect and work for these principles, to defend them in the Constituent Assembly, we will publicize your name, we'll help you to campaign, we'll tell people they must vote for you, no matter what party you belong to, no matter what your religion, whether you are Catholic, Protestant, spiritualist or atheist.'

Cardinal Leme – who at that time was the only cardinal in Brazil and was considered head of the Church – asked all the bishops to do this in their respective dioceses. So the Church represented a considerable force in the elections. The candidates – all the candidates – paid great attention to the League, and willingly accepted its programme. They more or less had to if they wanted to be elected. They had to make sure that their names would be included among those the League publicized in the newspapers and on the radio.

It was only in my part of the world, in Ceará, that things happened differently. I was at a Catholic education conference in Rio de Janeiro, when I suddenly got a telegram from my archbishop in Fortaleza telling me to return immediately, by air. That was the first time I had travelled by air. When I got back, he said: 'You know this system of the Catholic Electoral League won't work here. It's too vague. If we recommend just any candidate from any party, simply because he has agreed in theory to support our principles in the Constituent Assembly, we can't be sure of the result. So what we've done here is draw up a list of our candidates for the governor, senators and representatives for Ceará. I want you to set off immediately, go to all the towns and villages in Ceará and tell people that the Church has its own list of candidates, and these are the candidates they must vote for.'

You have to understand that at that time, and even today to some extent, I had absolute respect for my superiors. I didn't argue. It was my bishop speaking . . .

You argued with your Rector, in the seminary . . .

Yes, but you see a bishop . . . Each of us is one with Christ: but I felt that only one man, the Holy Father, was the true Vicar of Christ, and that bishops, like the Pope, were the living presence of Christ in their dioceses. So even if I did argue, my bishop must always have the last word.

So off I went from town to town. I stuck rigidly to the itinerary and the timetable I had been given. I said exactly what the archbishop had told me to say. I wasn't there to talk about the people's problems. I wasn't even there to explain the principles that the Church was proposing for the new constitution. The only thing that mattered was to say to the people: 'Here are our candidates; these are the candidates you have to vote for.' The result was that in Ceará all of the Church's candidates – and only the Church's candidates – were elected. The candidates who weren't on our list, in the end, didn't have a chance.

In other words the clergy exercised complete control over the electorate.

Yes, at least in Ceará.

The most astonishing thing is that the Archbishop of Fortaleza was the only one in the whole of Brazil who took advantage of it.

Yes. But I think the ones who followed Cardinal Leme's instructions were wiser. My bishop had enormous problems afterwards, because once his candidates were elected they didn't owe the Church any loyalty, and they didn't keep their promises.

And there was another, very unpleasant, development. Throughout the electoral campaign, in order to excuse and justify my intervention, I had repeated over and over again that I personally had no political ambitions, that I was not seeking any personal gain. But no sooner was it all over than the new governor, delighted with his campaign manager, insisted that the archbishop allow Father Helder to be appointed Director of the Department of Education, which was attached to the Secretariat of the Interior and of Justice.

This time I argued with the archbishop every step of the way: 'Forgive me! It's impossible for me to accept this appointment. I told everyone that I had no political ambition, that I would not accept any benefits from the election. It would be a terrible humiliation for me. Please don't insist! In any case, I'm not an expert in education; I'm not at all suitable.' 'But you are: you're padre to the Teachers' Association – you even set up the Teachers' Association. You've given courses in pedagogy and psychology . . . No, there's no question about it. You are the obvious man for the position. It is God's will, because . . . it is your bishop's will.'

I went to see the governor, and said: 'I agree to obey my bishop's command on one absolute condition: and that is that in the field of education which you want me to supervise neither you yourself, nor I, obviously, will ever allow partisan considerations or preferences to intervene. In other words no one will ever be transferred, or penalized, because he is opposed to the government or because he voted against your list, which was also the Church's list.' Perhaps I should explain that partisan politics is a terrible problem here, particularly in small towns. Anyone who hasn't voted for the government is liable to be silenced – simply dismissed. That's why I was absolutely determined that my condition should be stated and agreed on from the start.

The governor did agree, and for the first few months everything went smoothly. From time to time the governor would tell me that he wanted to have such and such a person dismissed or transferred, and I was able to refuse: 'No, I've investigated the matter: this person is a conscientious worker and a good teacher. His personal life and his opinions are irrelevant. We will not allow partisan politics to intervene.' And so on. But after a while the governor ceased to respect our agreement. He had the power to make decisions independently of me, because the Secretaries of the Interior and of Justice were superior to the Director of the Education Department. So I resigned.

From the beginning I had been in close touch with the great Brazilian pedagogue Lourenço Filho, who had been summoned to Ceará from São Paulo in 1922 to take charge of the Department of Education, and establish the New School there.

What was the New School exactly?

The New School was based on a new kind of teaching. It was influenced by the ideas of Decroly in Europe, and John Dewey in the United States. Lourenço Filho realized the significance of the new movement: he envisaged not only a more vital, active form of teaching, but also schools with more sense of community, where parents played a more significant part. Filho invited me to meet him in Rio de Janeiro.

Forgive me, but before we move on to your career in education could we just talk a little more about relations between the Church and politics?

You said that the Catholic Electoral League presented candidates with a certain number of principles. What were the principles? What was the Church's constitutional programme in 1934?

The candidates had to undertake to respect the indissolubility of marriage, in other words not to legalize divorce; or to guarantee optional religious instruction in schools . . .

> In all schools, public and private?

Yes, and not just Catholic instruction, but whatever religious instruction the parents wished, in accordance with the programmes and conditions defined by the leaders of the various faiths.

The Catholic Electoral League also called for the establishment of padres in the army. All of this reflected the Church's preoccupation with morality, and also its preoccupation with being recognized as a presence in public institutions. But it's true that the League dedicated a whole chapter of its programme to the right to work, which had not been included in the 1891 constitution, but was introduced in 1934.

> The Catholic Electoral League proved very effective in the Constituent elections in 1934. What about afterwards?

Afterwards, under Vargas' dictatorship, it became practically impossible to repeat the operation. And today the constitution prohibits the formation of electoral leagues.

> I once saw a document dating from 1947 or 1948 in which the Catholic Electoral League – the same one – was redefining its aims. So it did at least survive the Vargas period.

Yes, probably. I can't remember exactly. But it wasn't the same any more. What strikes me now when I look back at the heyday of the League is that it was not concerned with defending the rights of the individual, or the oppressed, but only with defending morals and religion. That was the attitude of the times...

> After the elections the Catholic Electoral League was demobilized; but Cardinal Leme remained. How

did the Church, as represented by the Cardinal of Rio, get on with Getúlio Vargas?

Cardinal Leme had a very special way of handling politicians: through their wives or mothers.

I remember an incident involving Vargas' Minister of Foreign Affairs, for instance, Oswaldo Aranha. After the war he was elected president of the United Nations Organization, and it was while he was president that the UN voted to create the State of Israel. Aranha is very popular in Israel.

He came from the same region as Vargas, Rio Grande do Sul. His mother was a great lady, a matriarchal figure. All the politicians in Rio Grande do Sul respected her, even the ones in the opposition. She was really 'somebody'. Cardinal Leme was a friend of hers. Whenever he wanted Vargas to do something for him, he would simply let Oswaldo Aranha's mother know. That was his way of conducting politics. 'I know the power of women,' he used to say.

One day Getúlio Vargas received a proposal for a law in favour of divorce. 'I'm quite prepared to sign it,' he said, 'as long as two other people sign it first: Cardinal Leme and Senhora Aranha!'

Wasn't it because of this proposed law in favour of divorce that Cardinal Leme organized a massive demonstration of Catholics around Our Lady of Aparecida, to impress Vargas and his government?

Yes, there was something like that and it was very typical of those times. The Virgin Mary is really beloved by all the Brazilian people. Every region has its own name for her. But the great national sanctuary is at Aparecida, near São Paulo. There is a long history of the Virgin appearing there: an enormous church has been built in Her honour – it's wonderful – and people go there on pilgrimages all the year round.

So on this occasion, when Cardinal Leme felt the Church was being challenged, he had the idea of taking the statue of Our Lady of Aparecida on a journey all over the country. In every diocese it was greeted by enormous crowds, and when it reached Rio de Janeiro the whole city came out to celebrate. There were more people in the streets than at Carnival time! It was a national demonstration of faith, calculated to show the head of state, the government and the politicians the extent of the Brazilian people's devotion to the Church. Everyone had to be there: it was a question of faith!

> A sort of referendum.

Yes, exactly. It was really extraordinary to see these immense crowds, a sea of people. Of course, Cardinal Leme understood the people very well. He knew how to talk to them. He was a remarkable orator. He spoke in short sentences that made an immediate impact and stirred the imagination. Vargas and all the politicians respected him enormously because . . .

> Do you mean they were afraid of him?

Because these were the electors he was speaking to. These gatherings exercised considerable moral pressure on the politicians.

> Could they be compared to the colossal demonstrations of the Marian Congregations, or the Tradition, Family, Property Movement that precipitated the downfall of João Goulart in 1964?

Yes. In 1964 people everywhere were being told that the Communist menace was at the door. Here in Pernambuco they were even saying that Communism was already in our midst, because there was a local deputy, Francisco Julião, who had been forming Peasants' Leagues, and a governor, Miguel Arraes, who was seen as a future Fidel Castro. These ideas were put about mainly by the press and by North American propaganda. The American priests who led the Crusade of the Rosary also helped to mobilize Catholics against Communism, by saying it was about to come to power. There were rumours everywhere. And everywhere the Church organized processions of the Blessed Virgin. The statue of Our Lady of Fatima was brought here and crowned with a crown of gold that had been blessed by the Pope, and so on. It was all popular psychology. Immense crowds gathered and filed past. For the Blessed Virgin and against Communism, which was always presented as the enemy of the family, property and religion ...

> And this time the bishops were no longer 'the challengers', the mobilizing force: they were really in a way outflanked by the people.

I would go so far as to say that at that time certain political and even, in the background, military forces were already at work. And they could count on the support of certain bishops. But when the supposed revolution took place it became obvious that it was largely supported by people who had been thrown into a state of panic by propaganda about the imminent danger of Communist domination!

> Was it to some extent this kind of outflanking by the people in 1964 that made certain bishops, yourself included, want to get closer to the people and to popular religion, to get a better understanding of the religious psychology of the masses?

No, no. Speaking for myself at least, the phenomenon you described first emerged when we began to investigate social problems and to realize that the major conflict was not that between Capitalism and Communism, between East and West. Capitalism exploited the East-West conflict for its own ends, presenting itself – as it still presents itself now in Brazil, in fact in the whole of Latin America – as the saviour of Christian civilization. That's total hypocrisy as the roots of Capitalism are entirely materialistic. It is irresponsible to make such claims. We wanted to face up to the important human problems. We wanted people to realize that within our own country and continent there is the scandal of internal colonialism; and that on an international level there is the scandal of rich countries who maintain their wealth by keeping poor countries in misery. To say or think that what led us to side with the oppressed and the people was out of political considerations, a fear of losing their support, a desire to preserve our influence over them – no, no, it's impossible, because it's untrue. Absolutely untrue.

Our main concern was to make sure that the people would no longer be exploited. We were aware that we ourselves had manipulated the people; we had used them to defend a certain kind of morality, to defend what we had called religious principles, to defend the family against divorce for instance, and religious teaching in schools, and the presence of padres in the army and in hospitals. We had been so blinded then by the need to maintain, sustain and support authority and social order that we couldn't see the terrible, cruel injustices that this authority and social order permitted. But as soon as we began to realize the truth and face up to it, we had to think and act in a different way.

And there were the encyclicals. If you look at the whole series of encyclicals, from Leo XIII to Paul VI, you find that each one is more stringent than the last on the subject of justice. But it's a pity . . . it's a pity that we Christians – Catholics and Protestants alike – are so intelligent, so strong when it comes to setting fine important principles down on paper, and so weak afterwards, so timid and fearful when it comes to enacting those principles. And it isn't only the resistance, the opposition, the pressure from governments that prevents us enacting, for example, the remarkable conclusions of the Second Vatican Council. Very often it's the cautious advice from within our own ranks: 'We must be patient! We mustn't go too fast!' The response to that must be: 'I'm sorry! But the principles are here, the conclusions are here. We have discussed them at great length. We have agreed on them and ratified them. And it's not true to say we want to go too fast. Latin America has been waiting for four and a half centuries. And Africa, and Asia . . . Why should we not preach revolution? Revolution to us doesn't mean violence and armed combat. It means the radical and swift change of unjust structures. It has nothing to do with the numerous revolutions Latin America has seen already, which have often resulted in a change of personnel, but never in a change of structures.'

We aren't preoccupied with tactics. When we began to investigate social problems we realized the importance and urgency of human advancement. Human advancement is not like the advancement of a civil servant, say, who wants to move up from category G to category H! There are hundreds of millions of people in the world who are living in sub-human conditions. It's true that only they can raise themselves up: we can't do it for them. But we can and we must help them and encourage them. And first we have to defend them, to make sure that they are at least given the opportunity to raise themselves to a human condition. If only we could all dedicate ourselves to the cause of human advancement . . .

I'll tell you what finally opened our eyes. On the one hand, the reality that appeared more and more brutal; on the other, the teaching of the Popes and the Church contained in the encyclicals and the Second Vatican Council. And then, the miracle of Pope John! How he reinforced our faith in the active presence of the Holy Spirit!

No one was expecting Pope John. Leo XIII, Pius X, Benedict XV, Pius XI, Pius XII . . . There we were, listening to the radio, and asking ourselves: 'Who will be elected, who will be chosen by Providence to follow this wonderful succession of pontiffs?' And we were told that a certain Angelo Roncalli had been elected. He had chosen to be called John XXIII. An old man . . .

In less than five years everything had changed, a complete revolution was under way. There's no human explanation. What a great day it was when this old man announced that the Holy Spirit had inspired him to summon an ecumenical council; and that he saw the reform of the Church as a preliminary step to the union of all Christians! A great event!

So you see there was a whole series of things that brought about our change of attitude. We couldn't remain any longer as we had been, tied to the social order, to political power and the State . . .

> But it seems to me that you yourself kept up that link with the State. For the twelve years during which you were Secretary of the Episcopal Conference of Brazil, you were the principal agent responsible for relations between the Church and State. You

negotiated and worked with each successive government, under Kubitschek, Quadros and Goulart.

Yes. Remember what I was saying to you about Saint
Augustine: I passed from the Integralist conception, which
more or less claimed to submit temporal power to spiritual
power, to the idea that the two powers – the two swords, as
they used to be called – are complementary and jointly
responsible for governing the world.

Since the early fifties I had felt the need for a Secretariat,
or some kind of body that could help bishops to cope with
their responsibilities. After the war Rome had created a great
many new dioceses in Brazil, which meant as many new
bishops. When a bishop is appointed, especially if he has a
large diocese, he immediately becomes absorbed with his
pastoral preoccupations and doesn't have the opportunity to
study, much less solve, important general problems. So I
presented to Monsignor Montini in Rome, and examined
with him, the urgent need for a conference of Brazilian
bishops, and also a Latin American Episcopal Council for
the whole continent.

I remember saying to Monsignor Montini: 'You know, we
have an opportunity in Brazil to establish an almost ideal
model of relations between Church and State. Catholicism
does not have the status of an official religion. But there is
great mutual respect between the Church and the government, and we work in close collaboration. An Episcopal
Conference would facilitate that collaboration enormously.'

Even before the Episcopal Conference was set up – under
the aegis of Catholic Action, and under the protection of the
apostolic nunciature – but especially afterwards, we arranged regional meetings of bishops to help them recognize
and understand the major social problems of their region.
There were meetings for the prelates of Amazonas, for the
bishops of the North-East, of the São Francisco valley, and so
on. We carried out this programme of awareness in a way
that seems curious today. We were able to call upon the best
consultants and experts from the various government
ministries, and together with them we looked for solutions

to the country's major problems.

I'll give you an example. Here in the North-East it was apparent that the gap, the distance that separated us from the industrialized South was getting bigger all the time. There was even a danger of a split or a separation between these two regions that were so different. So with the help of the government experts we were able to demonstrate that the federal funds coming to the North-East were being scattered and dispersed too widely, that there was no overall policy for the region's economy, and that above all there was no organization to supervise the development of the North-East. So it was really the Church that was responsible for the creation of SUDENE – Superintendence for the Development of the North-East.

And the government didn't stop at sending its best advisers to work with the bishops. The President of the Republic himself used to come to the closing sessions of the meetings. President Kubitschek, for example. But even before him I remember when Vargas was elected to the presidency in 1951, he insisted on sending a personal representative, a special representative of the government, to ensure that all the State apparatus was made available to us in preparation for the International Eucharistic Congress of 1954–5. Every door was opened to us, every facility was made available. That was how we were able to get a huge esplanade built across the bay right in the heart of Rio – the project was already under way, and we got it speeded up.

It makes me a little sad now to think of how we conceived of relations between the Church and the State in those days. It didn't occur to us that by working hand in hand with the government we were tacitly approving the established social order, and indirectly approving the injustices perpetuated by that order ...

> That's exactly what Carlos Lacerda reproached you with, on one occasion in an open letter that took up a whole page of the *Tribuna da Impresa*. He had criticized you for alienating the spiritual power of the Church by lending its security to the State and the current regime. And if I remember rightly, the reply

> you gave then was not quite the same as it would be
> today ...

No, of course! But we were on the move. Even if we weren't
yet capable of seeing that we were involuntarily lending
security to an unjust regime, at least we were ready to face
up to the real and important problems of the regions, the
country and the people.

> It must have been a piece of cake, if I may say so,
> dealing with the Brazilian heads of state at that time:
> people like Kubitschek and Quadros were them-
> selves very keen to collaborate with the Church,
> weren't they?

Yes, absolutely. Kubitschek more than anyone. He played
an important part in the history of development. Ah! The
magic word: 'development'! For a long time we used to talk
about 'progress'. But that expression got so worn out that we
had to find another one. So people started saying 'development'. I was shaken at first. There were developed countries
and there were under-developed countries. The United
Nations always preferred the euphemism: 'less developed',
or 'in the process of development'. So *we* were under-
developed! We must work towards full development at
once!

At that time I was convinced that organizations like
SUDENE could really help us to change the social structures.
The first superintendent in charge of SUDENE was Celso
Furtado, a very well-qualified man. He devised a plan for a
whole series of radical reforms, beginning with agricultural
reform. But he soon discovered that he had neither the
support nor the political means necessary to carry out these
reforms, particularly the agricultural reform. So he turned
his attention to the industrialization of the North-East, in
the belief that this would bring about essential changes.

Sadly, the noble idea of development became degraded,
robbed of its original meaning. Very soon in Brazil, as with
everywhere else, development came to mean simply economic growth: people didn't see that it brought profit only
to the privileged classes, and that it was achieved at the cost

of further proletarization of the masses. That's why we now prefer, in Brazil and in the rest of Latin America, to speak of 'liberation', and why we try to ensure that this word does not become degraded as the word 'development' became degraded. It didn't take long for people to forget the true definition of development, the one given by François Perroux and quoted by Paul VI: 'the development of the whole man and of all men'. The whole man and all men . . .

> Since 1964 the Church has moved from collaboration with the government into opposition.

How can I explain? . . . You might well think that bishops who took the side of the people, the oppressed, the silent majority, would inevitably be opposed to the army and the government. But it doesn't work like that. God sees what we are trying to do and the people see it too. The problem was that the so-called revolution was content with the kind of development that meant economic growth for the privileged classes, and that it was afraid of human advancement – although the official speeches denied it. As soon as we began to campaign for human advancement, to arouse the critical consciousness of the people, we were immediately denounced as 'subversives' and 'Communists'.

I once put the question directly to a general: 'Why do you call me a Communist? Why do you persecute not just Dom Helder but everyone who is working and fighting for human advancement, calling them Communists and subversives?' And he replied: 'It's very simple. It's much easier and quicker to open people's eyes than to carry out reforms, do you know that? If you do know it, and yet you continue to open people's eyes and spread ideas about reforms that cannot be carried out immediately, you are obviously an agitator and a subversive. Communism takes advantage of this newly-aroused critical consciousness: so you are doing the work of Communists.' And I said to him: 'You call me an agitator, a subversive? The very situation in which the people live is subversive!'

In fact they know very well that we are not Communists, and that we are not doing the work of Communists. The work of Communists is being done by all those who are helping to bring profit to the privileged classes, and proletarization to the masses. And by those who call the true defence of human rights 'Communism'. Because the people will listen to their propaganda and say to themselves: 'So that's Communism! Well then Communism is a wonderful thing! We must all support the Communists!'

> You began to say something about Kubitschek. Perhaps you would like to say more about him?

Kubitschek was the man who threw out the incredible, spectacular challenge: 'Fifty years in five years.' Five years is the presidential term of office. Fifty years was how far Brazil lagged behind the developed world. Kubitschek conceived of a nationwide development plan: he assembled a team of experts, and he put the plan into operation.

But Kubitschek and all his experts, and all of us in the Church, were extremely naive: we weren't aware, for instance, of the power of the multinationals. We weren't aware of the alliance that already existed between the huge multinational corporations that were offering us aid and the privileged classes inside Brazil. Without wanting to we merely added to the burden of oppression, reinforced the unjust structures under which the people suffered. That's why we must think now about liberation and help to bring about the liberation of the people.

7

A CIVIL SERVANT PRIEST

A large part of your life, from 1931 to 1947 or 1948, was devoted to educational work. You were Secretary of Education for Integralist Action in Ceará, then Director of the Department of Education in the State of Ceará, and then in Rio de Janeiro you worked as technical adviser at the Ministry of Education, and were a member of the Higher Council of Education. A whole career in itself, almost. Did you have a particular personal interest in education and in teaching? Did it come from your mother, perhaps? And why, in 1936 or 1937, did you take an examination to qualify as a technical civil servant?

This was another process of evolution for me. I progressed from a narrow, limited view of education to a wider, more profound vision. At first, and even after I went to Rio de Janeiro, I was concerned only with reforming teaching methods. I simply had no conception of the real problems, the important problems, of educating the individual. I admit that now with humility.

When I first went to Rio de Janeiro, at the invitation of Lourenço Filho, I worked for a short time at the Institute of Education. But then Everardo Backheuser, who had founded the Catholic Confederation of Education and was now Director of the Institute of Teaching Research in the former federal capital, appointed me head of his Organization and

Planning section. In those days there were a hundred and fifty thousand pupils in the primary classes of the state schools of Rio de Janeiro, not counting those who attended evening classes. I was asked to make intelligence level tests. So there was Father Helder, busy devising examinations and objective methods of assessing the capacity and progress of these hundred and fifty thousand pupils. And I was quite happy at the time with this superficial approach to education.

When the Minister of Education first organized a competitive examination for the post of technical adviser in education, I went to see Cardinal Leme and said: 'Your Eminence, when I arrived here I was given the title technical adviser in education even though I had neither qualifications nor experience in that field. I have been given responsibility, and teachers have made me welcome in all the schools. Now that this competition is being held I feel morally obliged to enter for it, to undergo the test.'

The thesis I submitted for the examination was a disgrace: it was terrible. I haven't kept a single copy of it, and I sincerely hope no one else ever finds one. It was a study of all the tests I had prepared and carried out in the schools in the federal district. I was naive enough to believe that it was possible to find an objective means of evaluation.

So as to be fair to everyone?

Yes, to be fair to everyone. But of course everybody knows that the most important things about a human being cannot be measured objectively. Take the simple matter of language: there's no objective way of measuring someone's capacity for literary creation. How can you pick out a future writer by means of objective tests?

It was the same when I was a member of the Higher Council of Education. The work we did was far less grand than the name 'Higher Council' suggests. It was rather like directing traffic, in fact. For example: there was a plan to set up a school of philosophy in Piaui. It had to comply with a number of conditions. The dossier was prepared in Piaui, and then sent to the Higher Council of Education in Rio. So the Council met to examine the project – in other words, to make sure that everything was as it should be, that all the regulations were being observed. We began by studying the building plans, then the equipment, and finally we got around to the curriculum. And then we could say: 'Yes, this school can be set up', or 'No, in order to set up this school, this or that condition has to be fulfilled'. And that was what we did.

Well in any case I passed the examination, so I was now officially a technical adviser in education. What a title! . . . I remember once an old American professor was invited to give us a series of lectures, and he drew up a register of the audience himself. He asked everyone in turn: 'What is your name? What is your profession?' When he got to me I replied naturally 'technical adviser in education'. And with a single gesture he opened my eyes to the absurdity of that title: '. . . in education?' he said, and spread his arms wide with astonishment. He was right: how could anyone claim to be expert in every different sector of the vast field of education? No doubt you could master one aspect or another: but the whole of education!

Fortunately the Lord was patiently preparing the way for me. It was at this time that I immersed myself in the *favelas* of Rio de Janeiro, and got to know the misery that was there. And later, at the meetings of the bishops of Amazonas, the North-East and the Central-West, I discovered new and far more profound dimensions in educational problems.

Gradually we priests and bishops began to ask ourselves questions. Although primary education was State-controlled, most secondary and higher education took place in private schools – which were largely Catholic schools. What had we done with the sons of the rich who attended our schools and universities? What kind of education had we given them? Had we taken advantage of their presence in our schools and universities to acquaint them with important social problems, problems of justice? No doubt we were very well qualified to teach them what we had learned ourselves of Greek and Latin humanism. But was that true humanism? All too often we had failed to realize that educating and developing people involves awakening the human spirit, widening the human vision, expanding the human heart and overcoming selfishness. But the misery we found in the *favelas*, and the social problems we discovered through Catholic Action and through the bishops gradually revealed to us the requirements of a true education.

> And this gradual discovery led to the Movement for Basic Education, the MEB?*

Yes. But it's difficult to keep going in a straight line when you're cutting a new path. The Lord helps us, but our own weakness trips us back into the old ruts...

The Movement for Basic Education was a step forward, yes – an enormous step compared to what had been achieved before. I remember when my brother, Dom Távora – we worked and thought together – wrote a letter to the president elect, Janio Quadros, while he was travelling in Europe, to propose setting up the Movement for Basic Education. He put it to him like this: 'The State hasn't the means to educate the whole Brazilian population on its own, has it? It can't build enough schools or employ enough teachers. It ought to take advantage of radio; but the government also hasn't the means to do that properly. You'd have to train tutors, and then they would have to be paid. The Church can help. It can mobilize religious commitment and provide tutors all over the country.'

The idea was to offer an integral education, to make people more aware. 'Alphabetization', as it was called, went hand in hand with 'consciousness raising'. The Movement for Basic Education represented real progress in education, both theoretical and practical. But we were still tied to the State.

> Would it have been conceivable otherwise?

Perhaps it wouldn't. But we should have the courage to keep the work of the Church separate from the politics of government, to make it quite clear that we do not condone its pretence of order.

* Movimento de Educação de Base.

> Yes, but at that time you didn't realize it was a 'pretence'.

You're right . . . it's always unfair to judge the past by present standards . . . But we should see the way the Lord is encouraging us to go, allowing us to go, helping us to go . . .

> There was a lot of discussion in Brazil in the thirties about the 'Pioneers' Manifesto'. I believe it was an expression of the New School movement that you have already mentioned. Did you agree with it?

That's another episode which I think was very unfortunate for the Church. It was a minor document: minor in the sense that it was concerned merely with problems of different methods of teaching, without going any further or deeper. But certain people in the Church, even well-informed, sensible people, saw signs of pragmatism and materialism in it; even Communism. Certainly they felt it reflected Watson's behaviourist ideas. And they launched a whole campaign against the 'Pioneers'.

I think I have already told you the story of a terrible, disgraceful incident I was involved in, at a Pioneers' conference in Ceará? I had agreed to give a lecture. I was quite well known in my own state, and the lecture theatre was full. There were people who were taking part in the conference and people who had come especially to hear me. I gave my lecture. There was thunderous applause. But when it died down I said: 'Friends! We don't belong here! I am leaving, and I want my friends to come with me!' The theatre emptied immediately: only the Pioneers were left. It was an act of sabotage, which the Confederation of Catholic Education had instructed me to carry out. Their methods were absolutely totalitarian.

Totalitarian methods were already quite common in those days. When I first went to Rio de Janeiro Vargas had just dismissed the mayor of the city, accusing him of having left-wing ideas and of being a Communist. He got rid of Anisio Teixeira, the Secretary of Education, for the same reason.

It was disgraceful: there weren't any Communists! Now when I am attacked, or when someone calls me a Communist, I often pray to the Lord: 'that this injustice done to me may be a small atonement for all those who have suffered at our hands.' I can understand how they felt.

> Would you be as critical of religious education as you are of general education? Didn't Cardinal Leme put you in charge of religious education for the archbishopric of Rio de Janeiro?

No, not exactly. When I arrived in Rio de Janeiro there was already a director of religious education. But as I was a 'technical adviser in education', you see, the cardinal appointed me 'technical director of religious education'! Can you imagine?

> And what did that involve, exactly?

I was to prepare a programme for modernizing religious education. That was my brief. In fact, once again, all it meant was devising new and more active methods. But there was the same blindness to the real requirements of a Christian education. Oh, if only we'd been able to understand and interpret religious events, and the living presence of Christ, to communicate to children, and young people, and adults, rich and poor alike, the terrific strength that can come from true religion. Think for instance of the Trinity and the wonderful story of the Creation: the Father who wants man to be co-creator with Him; the Son who began the great work of liberation and wants man to be His co-redeemer; and the Holy Spirit who calls for and requires our collaboration. I think that is true religion. If we had been able to communicate it through religious instruction, through the catechism, we could have changed many things. Personally I don't believe in the conversion of the bourgeois structures as such. Within the structures there are people who are hungry and thirsty for true Christianity. But I have to admit with humility that religious education at that time was also still at the beginning of a very long road.

> Were you aware of the developments that were taking place in Germany and France at the same time, the so-called biblical, liturgical and catechistic revivals?

Those movements didn't really have any effect on religious education in Brazil; but they did affect Catholic Action. The liturgical revival, for example, had a profound effect on us. And so did the biblical revival. They helped us to a better spiritual understanding of the Ecumenical Council.

> Did the revivals in Brazil stem from the European movements, or did they originate independently in Latin America?

No, it all came from Europe. I should explain perhaps that we are only now beginning to have the courage to allow ourselves, for instance, a certain degree of liturgical creativity. We always used to think, we priests and bishops, that nothing must be changed, not even the rubrics. The rubrics were sacred! I remember how we were taught to arrange our fingers during mass, after the consecration. That was sacred, too! And when a bishop was about to administer communion, the body of Christ, the communicant would first of all have to kiss his ring. Imagine that: first the ring, then the body of Christ! It was as if the respect due to the bishop and the communion service were placed on the same level of importance as the love of Christ! ...

> So what Pope John XXIII called *aggiornamento* began rather late in Brazil?

As I was saying, it's only now that we are beginning to have a little more courage in introducing reforms. This is unfortunately one of the human weaknesses of the Church: the confusion between the prudence of the Holy Spirit and the prudence of the flesh, human prudence. Under the influence of the Holy Spirit we may have remarkable courage for composing fine resolutions and drawing large conclusions. But afterwards we are tempted by prudence: 'We must be patient.' And what happens is that while the commissioners in Rome are busy making up rules and regulations for our lives, the young seminarists, the new priests, the laity, the people and Christian communities, go on ahead, far far ahead. If the advocates of prudence and patience were to take a trip around the world, they'd get an enormous shock. You can't regulate the Holy Spirit!

> When you were technical director of religious education you invented 'catechistical marathons'. What were they, exactly?

The catechistical marathon was another symptom of the narrowness I've already described. It was a competition based on the same kind of tests as I'd devised for primary schools. There were eliminating rounds in every diocese, then in every region, and eventually all the finalists were assembled in a huge hall in Rio de Janeiro in front of an enormous audience, and a jury. The competition consisted of a written examination and oral questions. The winner of the marathon won a trip to Europe...

> Have you read Ivan Illich's book, *Deschooling Society**?

You know ...

> Are you an Illich-ite, as it were?

Illich and I are brothers. I respect him enormously, I admire him. We are very very close friends. But I think we have different...utopias. When Illich attacks schools, or hospitals, or medicine, it seems to me what he really wants is to overthrow all structures. When I say we have different utopias, I mean that his idea of making life more human again seems to involve rejecting society completely and returning more or less to a natural state. I personally believe that the Lord has entrusted us with the task of subduing nature, and completing the process of creation. That's why He has made us intelligent and creative. So I am not afraid of progress, I am not afraid of technology. What I won't accept is that

* *Deschooling Society* (1971) John Calder Ltd, London and Harper & Row, New York.

technological progress should bring benefits only to a small privileged group that's growing smaller all the time. What I hope for is the socialization of technological progress, in the service of all mankind.

> You're closer to Teilhard de Chardin than to Ivan Illich?

Yes, I'm a disciple of Teilhard ...

> Totally?

Yes, totally and absolutely.

> Have you been a disciple ever since you began to read his work?

No. I think I was a disciple even before I read him.

> Through poetry?

Through inspiration. When the Lord breathes a thought into the world, it germinates here and there, apparently without communication.

But really I rely a great deal on Teilhard. We have the same utopia, we are going in the same direction. Like him I believe that humanity is moving towards a higher level of consciousness. In every race, every religion, every human group, there are minorities which in the West I call 'Abrahamic' – and which I'd find another name for if I went to the East – minorities that are very different from one another, but have as a common denominator the same hunger and thirst for a world that is freer, more just, more brotherly: and when I see the vitality of all these groups, I have enormous confidence in the future! ...

> During the long period when you were a 'technical adviser in education', you really lived the life of a civil servant, a bureaucrat, among offices and pieces of paper. It can hardly have been what you had in mind when you decided to become a priest?

Absolutely: and the real sacrifice came after I had passed the examination to become an official 'technical adviser in education', and went to work in a government ministry. That was real bureaucracy. I had exactly the same duties as the other civil servants. We clocked on in the morning and we clocked off at night. It was really like being a worker priest, except that I was actually a civil servant priest.

But fortunately I got on well with all my colleagues, including the director, who used to confide in me and tell me all his problems; and I got on well with my colleagues' wives and children. I was almost like a spiritual adviser to the ministry. But the work itself . . . It was the worst sort of bureaucracy. I received documents, I examined them, I prepared notes, suggestions for answers or decisions, and passed them on to the minister.

The minister was Gustavo Capanema: a man of great sensibility and vision, who always had the courage of his convictions. He had appointed the greatest living Brazilian writer as his principal private secretary: Carlos Drummond de Andrade. He was a friend – patron, almost – of our greatest painter, Portinari, perhaps the greatest Brazilian painter of all time. He was a highly cultured man.

One day I went to Cardinal Leme and said: 'Your Eminence, it was I who asked your permission to enter for the examination to become technical adviser in education, because I felt I had a moral obligation to prove myself. But now I think I have proved myself. I have worked my way through practically the whole profession: I was a municipal civil servant in Rio de Janeiro, a provincial civil servant in Ceará, and now I am a federal civil servant at the ministry and even a member of the Higher Council for Education. I have done my best to profit from this experience as a civil servant priest. And now I am asking your permission to hand in my resignation. My work does not need to be done by a priest and I'm doing a layman's job, when a layman could do it just as well, if not better than I.'

But Cardinal Leme would not allow me to resign. 'The Church needs you to be where you are, among people who have stopped practising religion, who never have occasion

to see a priest. You are called to the apostolate of presence.'
He also said: 'You know that people often judge religion by
the priests they know. So stay where you are. Make the
sacrifice. Accept it with humility. This is the mission that the
Church has entrusted you with, for the time being.'

So I stayed. When Cardinal Jaime de Barros Camara
succeeded Cardinal Leme all the priests in the diocese had
to go and be presented to him and describe to him what they
were doing. I told him exactly what had happened to me,
and he too asked me to stay on at the ministry and in the
Higher Council. But finally I insisted: 'Your Eminence,
forgive me! I see and feel that there are so many other
important tasks for me to perform that are specifically the
work of a priest!' And he gave me permission to resign.

> As a civil servant were you getting a salary?

Yes.

> Did you live on your salary, or did you have any
> other income?

No, I lived on my salary, and used it for helping people
around me.

One of my brothers had come to Rio de Janeiro. He was
suffering from cirrhosis of the liver and eventually I had to
take him to hospital – to the hospital where I was padre. He
was very ill: but the doctors were wonderful. He stayed
there for more than a month and he lived for another eight
years after that.

He was five or six years older than I. He had been religious as a child: he'd been baptized, taken communion,
and gone to a school run by Marists. But afterwards, he said,
he had lost his faith completely.

So we lived together in a house I had rented in Rio de
Janeiro, with one of our sisters who had never married.
Every time I went out to celebrate mass and preach a
sermon he used to ask me: 'What are you going to say today?'
And I would tell him very simply what I had in mind,
without in any way wanting to preach to him or force him
to accept what I said. He never made any comment.

After eight years, when he realized that he was about to die, he sent for me and said, with immense humility: 'I know that you are more intelligent than I am, and far better educated. I trust you completely. I've never seen any inconsistency between your life and your faith. So tell me, do you think it's possible to believe by proxy, to take advantage of the faith of another person whom you believe in? I believe in your sincerity, but I have lost faith in God. Can I take communion on the strength of your faith?' And I told him: 'I am sure the Lord will reward you for your humility – I have no doubt of it. I will give you communion, and the Lord will open your eyes.' 'No, not yet. I want to make my confession first.' 'Then I'll go and get a priest.' 'No, I want to confess to you.' So he made a very humble confession, and just as he received the body of Christ a light came into his eyes. It is a great joy to witness the dawning of that light! I've seen it many times in my life. And he said: 'I believe! I believe! And it isn't just because you believe: now I believe as well!' Half an hour later he died...

And so with Cardinal de Barros Camara's permission you put an end to your career in education.

Except that I remained a member of the Higher Council for Education. That wasn't really work; it was more of an honorary position.

8

IN PRAISE OF THE
OCCULT APOSTOLATE

Was it at this time that you discovered what I believe you later called the 'occult apostolate'?

The occult apostolate? Oh, that's another chapter!...

One day Cardinal Leme sent me a message via Father Franca to say he wanted me to be a professor at the Catholic University he had decided to found. 'But Father Franca, I can't possibly agree! I've always dreamed of a Catholic university in Brazil, but one where I would be a student! I could understand if the cardinal had said I should go and study under the foreign professors he is going to invite to establish the university, so that I can prepare myself thoroughly to one day become assistant to a professor, and then perhaps take a doctorate and apply for a professorship. But I simply can't become a professor at once! Can't you explain to the cardinal?' But Cardinal Leme was adamant: 'Universities have to start somewhere: I'll give you a doctorate.'

So I was obliged to become a teacher. I had to teach... general and specialized didactics! Can you imagine? General and specialized didactics!... For a time I also taught academic administration. Me!...

But before I did that Cardinal Leme asked me to teach in the Faculty of Letters that had been founded by Ursuline nuns. Apart from being technical director of religious education, I was to give a course in psychology to the teaching nuns. My job was to help them understand their pupils better, to understand life, and understand the world. I enjoyed that enormously. It was really educational work, and therefore appropriate work for a priest.

The cardinal insisted – no, he didn't insist, he asked me to accept a professorship in the Ursuline Faculty of Letters.

In my first class of students there was a young girl – well, I suppose she wasn't all that young: I think she was a little older than I. Her name was Virginia Côrtes de Lacerda. I immediately sensed in her an exceptional, rare intelligence. She used to read the Greek classics in the original – Euripides, Sophocles . . .

She soon became my friend as well as my student. We began to work together and study together. At first she was reluctant to take an active part in our religious observances; but it wasn't long before she returned to the House of the Lord with a sincere and warm devotion.

She began to celebrate mass and take communion with me every morning. The mass was always well prepared: I used to read to her all the meditations, all the thoughts, that I wrote down during my vigil, so that she could progress with me. I have kept a vigil every night since I was in the seminary, so that I could renew my union with Christ.

Virginia and I also used to read, read, read – anything that we thought might help us, whether in a directly spiritual way, or in a cultural way.

One day we came across a book called *The Apostolate of the Hidden Elite*, or something like that. Through reading it, we discovered the occult apostolate. I even drew up a rule for the occult apostolate. Of course we never intended to found a separate community: but in fact a whole group formed around us. We used to meet every Friday at Virginia's house. We would always discuss a religious book; and often we would listen to music. Then we decided to go travelling – through thought and prayer. We worked out an itinerary each month and travelled each day from one country to the next, one town to the next, always making sure that we were well-informed about the situation, and the problems, in each particular country and town. We travelled in Asia, and right across Africa. It certainly helped to prepare me for the real journeys the Lord had in store for me later.

Among the books that I exchanged with Virginia was the *Meditations of Father Joseph* – the little texts that I write during my nightly vigil, the texts that my Rector in the seminary, Father Dequidt, used to call my poetry.

One day as I was leaving my spiritual director, Father Franca, he said to me: 'Have you nothing more you want to say?' I smiled: 'I imagine you have something more you want to ask me.' And he said: 'Father Joseph, who are you exactly?' And I smiled again. Someone had obviously told him about my writings: and I knew that Virginia was one of the few people who were familiar with Father Joseph. 'May I see the meditations?' he asked. I explained to Father Franca that I usually destroyed them as I thought of these meditations as like flowers that bloomed, which were offered as a gift, and then must fade. So he asked me to promise never to destroy them in future. 'If one or another of them seems to you to be kept secret, mark it; but don't destroy any of them. Give them to someone to look after – Virginia, for example.'

Father Franca was very fond of Virginia. But she died very suddenly of a heart attack. For eighteen hours she didn't recognize anyone, and couldn't speak. Of course we knew that for her it was the beginning of the true life; but her death was very hard for us.

Later we discovered to our surprise that before her death Virginia had carefully collected together all the things I had given her: letters, books, the *Meditations of Father Joseph*, wrapped them in a big parcel and sent them with a letter to one of our closest friends. When the friend told me I said perhaps it would be best to destroy them all.

She didn't argue: she agreed to destroy the whole correspondence bit by bit. But one day she began to read the *Meditations*; and in order to understand the *Meditations* she read the letters. After that she refused to destroy any more. She kept everything. She was also a member of the occult apostolate group.

I'm still not sure that I quite understand what the 'occult apostolate' was. It sounds almost like a secret society . . .

Oh, no, it was nothing like that! . . .

When it comes to faith, you know, the essence, the vital principle, is invisible. If somebody asked you to describe this room we are in, for example, you could talk about the walls, the things hanging on the walls, the table, the hammock. But you would be omitting the essence, the God who is within you and within me. The essence can't be pinned down.

It's the same with the external apostolate – the visible apostolate, if you like. The most intelligent, educated, zealous – apostolic – apostle, no matter how effective he may be, is no more than a minuscule drop in the ocean. Because the 'ocean' is not just our world, it is the universe, the whole of creation. And it isn't just the brief moments that we spend on this earth, it is the millennia that stretch from the creation into eternity.

So the Lord helped us to discover the hidden, occult dimension of the apostolate, and the way He expects us to co-operate with it, through humility. Without humility, and without love, we can't move a single step along the path of the Lord. The Lord makes big things out of little ones. Without humility you might look down from the height of perfection and simply not understand, or begin to imagine, the miracles that Christ performs with human weakness.

We must love small humiliations. An example of this could be if you work at something with total dedication, and all your intelligence, and love, and your work is received coldly and indifferently, with no acknowledgement of the fact that your heart is in it. It happens sometimes.

The Lord helped me to discover that it is impossible to achieve true humility without major, large-scale humiliations.

I experienced my first major humiliation when I was in the seminary. I think I may have told you the story already. At the time there was a woman – a teacher at the teachers' training college in Fortaleza – who was writing articles for the local newspaper which I thought smacked of materialism. I showed the articles to my Rector and he gave me permission to reply to them. So then I wrote some articles too, which were very cruel: 'Materialism in the teachers' training college!' When I think about them now I feel ashamed. What did I know of this materialism I was denouncing? There was a whole debate about it. Everyone in the seminary was reading my articles, and without realizing it I became terribly proud. I was convinced that the whole town was passionately involved in the argument.

After my fifth article appeared I received a summons from the Vicar General of the diocese, who lived in the seminary. His name was Monsignor Tabosa Braga – a very holy man. The archbishop was away, and so he was in charge of the diocese. As I left the study room to go and see him I was thinking: 'Perhaps Monsignor Tabosa wants to congratulate me on my articles. Who knows? Perhaps he'll ask me to write an article every day. Perhaps he's going to offer me my own column in the Catholic newspaper.'

When I went into his room he was holding my articles in his hand. 'Is it true that you wrote these articles?' I had signed them with a pseudonym, Alceu da Silveira. 'Yes, Monsignor!' I said proudly. 'Yesterday you wrote your last article!' 'But Monsignor! I don't understand! Have you read what this teacher has written? There's another article today! I must defend the faith!' But he simply repeated: 'Yesterday you wrote your last article. May God bless you.'

When I left the Vicar General's office I was in the throes of a violent conflict. I was eighteen years old. The Tempter breathed in my ear: 'Ha ha! That's what they're like, these churchmen! You know very well that the Vicar General is the brother-in-law of the teacher who wrote the articles! Make no mistake: this is just a beginning. Far worse things will happen to you later on. You've seen nothing yet!' My mind was in violent conflict.

I was just passing the chapel. I went in. The Lord was there. There was a statue of the Virgin Mary, and I prayed: 'Dear Mother, I won't leave this place until I have overcome the temptation. I feel that I have reached the crossroads. If my pride wins the struggle I know that I may lose my vocation and even my faith. I won't leave this place until I am at peace again.'

And then the conflict returned. I couldn't keep still, I paced about, it was terrible. It lasted more than an hour.

Then I remembered that it was Saint Martha's day, the twenty-ninth of July, and I thought of the Gospel: 'Martha, Martha, you are concerned with so many things. Only one is necessary: the Lord.' And immediately I was at peace. My eyes were opened and I said to myself: 'Helder! You are about to take the tonsure and prepare yourself for the priesthood. Are you going to prepare yourself in hatred? Because there is hatred in the articles you have written: hatred and pride. Is that how you are preparing for the priesthood?' It was really total acceptance of my humiliation.

When I came out of the chapel I was singing for joy: and all my fellow students were there waiting for me. The Rector had told them what had happened, and they were all ready to protest on my behalf against the Vicar General. There were even some of the seminary priests there in the background. But I said to them: 'Brothers, please be good enough to listen to me. I must tell you what has happened, and what has happened to me.' I told them everything in detail, from my meeting with the Vicar General to my conversion.

You know, even today, some of the most wonderful blessings I receive are granted to me on Saint Martha's day or during the seven days that follow. When you give very little things, really, you get miracles in return. And that's what the occult apostolate is: the Lord will match any little trifles that we manage to offer Him.

I suffered another great humiliation during the Second Vatican Council, and after it. We were all talking at the time about the need for a poor and serviceable Church. But I hadn't yet realized that true poverty is not the kind we choose ourselves.

The poverty that each of us needs at every stage in his life is chosen by the Lord ...

When I returned to Brazil after the Council was over I was thinking in terms of a poverty that involved getting rid of money. I didn't know and didn't understand, that the wealth the Lord wanted to relieve me of was prestige. I enjoyed a considerable reputation in my own country. I was on intimate terms with all sorts of important people: with the president, the ministers, the mayor of Rio de Janeiro. People talked about me, my photo appeared in all the newspapers and magazines. I had programmes on radio and television that were very popular. The Lord discovered the desire for poverty in the depths of my being, and undertook to snatch from me this wealth of prestige. Overnight I was reduced to nothing, less than nothing.

But still there were vicious campaigns against me, campaigns of calumny and slander. It was still not enough. The government realized that in a country like Brazil such campaigns and attacks merely keep the victim in the public eye. So it imposed silence. Today Dom Helder no longer enjoys even the fame of a victim, or a culprit; he has fallen into silence, like a tomb.

But I still have my international reputation... I don't know, I don't know when or how the Lord will snatch from me this last visible sign of wealth...

9

WE DON'T REALLY KNOW
WHAT WAR MEANS

Dom Helder, I'd like to go back a little way. There is
one page in history that we cannot pass over in
silence. How did the Second World War affect
Brazil, and what was your attitude to it? Not just
your own, but the attitude of the Brazilian people?
Because Brazil did take part in the war, didn't it?

Yes, Brazil took part in the war.

And on the side of the democracies, not the dictatorships, even though Brazil itself was under the dictatorship of Vargas at the time?

Yes. During the initial phase of the war Vargas supported
the Germans, and made preparations to join in on their side.
He certainly supplied them with raw materials.

There was definitely a minority in Brazil that supported
Hitler's Germany. It was mainly people who had never got
over Integralism. The most loyal Integralists were in favour
of Hitler, but more important, they were opposed to the
United States, and American democracy and liberalism.
But in general, most Brazilians supported the Allies.

We did take part in the war, but we never really experienced the horror of modern warfare. In one sense we
actually profited from the war. The warring nations needed
raw materials. So for countries like Brazil, who had raw
materials to sell, it was a great opportunity! Sell, sell, sell!

That's one of the terrible things about war . . . War finds natural allies in those who profit from it . . . In Brazil it meant more industrialization, mainly in the South, in the area around São Paulo. We could no longer import manufactured goods. So Vargas was able to impose conditions on the countries who needed our raw materials so that new industries were created in Brazil.

We had taken part in the First World War as well: we sent a boatload of troops to Europe. But before it got across the Atlantic an epidemic of Spanish 'flu broke out on board. Many of the soldiers died, though not in combat. Towards the end of the Second World War a Brazilian expeditionary force fought alongside the Americans against German troops in Italy. Its greatest victory was at Monte Castelo. Several hundred Brazilian soldiers were killed in the battle. They were buried at first in Italy; but later their remains were brought back to Rio de Janeiro, and a monument was erected there in memory of the battle.

But despite that, we can't really say that we know what modern warfare means. Many young Europeans have never experienced war; but their parents have lived through one, and their grandparents two. You know what it's like to go to bed at night knowing that you'll probably be awakened by sirens, aeroplanes, bombs. That's an experience we've never had.

> Does that mean that the prospect of a Third World War is not so totally horrific to Brazilians as it is to Europeans?

Brazilians who read newspapers and magazines, listen to the radio and watch television, have a pretty good idea of what war means. We see battles, bomb attacks, ruins, people wounded and dead. But I'm sure there is an enormous difference between reading about, seeing, and even hearing war – because you can hear aeroplanes approaching, bombs exploding, the wounded screaming – and the experience of living through it. You can't really imagine what it's like. For some people it probably seems like some kind of show.

But in Brazil like everywhere else there are informed and lucid minorities who know perfectly well that with modern weapons – nuclear, biological and chemical weapons – man has the appalling ability to destroy all life on earth. There are some people who understand that perfectly well.

10

LISTEN TO THE VOICE
OF THY PEOPLE

> Just after the war, in 1947, you set up a national
> secretariat for Catholic Action in Brazil. I believe
> this represented a very important stage in your
> journey – and not just your own personal journey.
> Nevertheless, Catholic Action already existed. What
> difference did a national secretariat make?

In 1916, when the future Cardinal Leme was Archbishop of
Olinda and Recife, he published an open letter which became famous. He accused Brazilian Catholics of being an
inert majority, of not putting their faith into practice, of not
being committed. Even then he was thinking and talking
about the apostolate of the laity. He was definitely one of the
forerunners and pioneers of Catholic Action. When he went
to Rio de Janeiro he founded a Catholic Confederation,
which consisted of ten committees representing all the lay
associations and activities. He also formed a group of
Catholic intellectuals, and University Action – which was a
sort of mother, or grandmother, to Catholic University
Youth.

When Pius XI officially authorized Catholic Action, the
cardinal immediately set about organizing it, and included
it – with an eleventh committee – in the Catholic Confederation. In 1934 the four 'branches' of Catholic Action –
for men, women, boys and girls – were officially constituted
in Brazil.

During my first years in Rio de Janeiro I was not directly involved in Catholic Action. It wasn't until 1946 that Cardinal Camara – who had succeeded Dom Leme – asked me if I would help organize a National Study Week for Catholic Action. That was when I first became enthusiastic about the movement. And while I was working with the different sectors, particularly the women's organizations, I began to realize that Catholic Action could never assert itself on a national level without a central secretariat that could win the confidence of the bishops and unite all the branches.

In 1947 I was appointed Deputy Padre-General of Catholic Action. The Padre-General was Cardinal Camara himself.

> Were you the first priest to have the job of Deputy Padre-General?

Yes. My job was to see that the four branches operated smoothly. Although I was appointed by the Archbishop of Rio de Janeiro, my duties extended nationwide. I was Deputy Padre-General of *Brazilian* Catholic Action.

I remember one particular national meeting of Catholic Action, held at Belo Horizonte. The cardinal wasn't there. But the bishops who came to that meeting finally said: 'It's a vicious circle: you complain that you're not getting enough help from the dioceses; but the reason you aren't getting help from the dioceses is because you have no central secretariat that could be of use to the dioceses; and the reason you have no central secretariat is because you aren't getting help from the dioceses. So here is our challenge: if you undertake to organize yourselves, and set up an effective secretariat, then we will help you.'

When I got back to Rio I told the cardinal what the bishops had said, and he told me to go ahead: 'I give you my blessing: that's all I can give you.' So I went ahead. I raised a little money, and we rented eight rooms on the sixteenth floor of number eleven, Mexico Street.

From the beginning the secretariat enabled us to keep in touch with the whole country. We had the support of all the bishops connected with Catholic Action, as well as the Cardinal of Rio and the new Cardinal of São Paulo, Vasconcelos Motta. We also had the support of the Papal Nuncio, Monsignor Chiarlo. So even before the National Conference of Bishops was founded we were able to begin organizing the regional meetings of bishops which I told you about before, and to discover some of the major problems of the people.

At the same time, in Brazil as in other countries, the 'special' branches of Catholic Action were developing. The general Catholic Action organization was opening people's eyes to human problems; but specialized Catholic Action went much further: it took us right into the midst of the workers, peasants, students, and so on, operating on the basis of Cardijn's trilogy – see, judge, act. Long before the phrase was invented, we were busy with the task of 'consciousness raising'.

Of course we had problems. As soon as the privileged classes – those who exploit the people – see that they have been found out they begin to murmur until they accuse us outright: 'But you're changing religion! You're changing the Church! The Church has always been our friend. But now you're turning it against us! You're teaching people to hate the rich!'

> The specialized Catholic Action organizations in Brazil – particularly the movements in universities, among students and workers – seem to have become radical very quickly, so that by the sixties they were adopting policies that were officially socialist and revolutionary. How do you account for that?

One of the problems in Brazil is that the hierarchy of the Church has a rather . . . curious attitude to politics. When it's a matter of politics in the general sense of the word, in aid of the so-called common good, they say it is the Christian's duty to become involved as the Gospel requires him to. But at the same time the Church itself is afraid of becoming involved in party politics or taking any stand against the government or the established order.

> The Church prefers politics that unite to politics that divide ...

Yes, but that doesn't take account of the fact that if you are not on the side of the oppressed you are on the side of the oppressors. It is always very difficult to remain neutral. And in our case – particularly in the regions and sectors where injustice is most flagrant, neutrality is really impossible. Of course we have to be very careful that in bringing about the advancement of the oppressed we don't encourage them to imitate the only kind of advancement they have ever seen – to follow the example set by their oppressors. It's very tempting and very easy – as many so-called revolutions have demonstrated – to transform the oppressed into oppressors. It's far more difficult to denounce and combat injustice without preaching hatred, and becoming full of hatred yourself ...

But you have to understand that young people are very logical, very genuine. They aren't bothered about prudence, or nuances, or precautions. It's only normal for young people to be radical. Too often people forget their own youth. When the bishops and the priests and the padres get the young people together and show them the great encyclicals and the conclusions reached at the Second Vatican Council or at Medellín, the young people think these encyclicals and conclusions are meant to be put into practice. They can't understand why these wonderful ideas have to go through some long slow process before they can be applied. Fortunately, young people reject all this false prudence – which I'm sure Christ Himself is the first to reject. But it's the human weakness of the Everlasting Church ...

As time went on certain members of the hierarchy became obsessed with what they saw as the Marxist tendencies of the university groups and the student groups. I don't condemn anyone for it: I know the bishops were sincere. But that's the way it always is. If you take the encyclical *Populorum progressio* and try to put it into practice, you are a Marxist ...

My God! Marxism! ... And Medellín? ... In 1968 we held a meeting at Medellín in Colombia of bishops representing all the episcopal conferences of Latin America. You couldn't imagine a more official sort of meeting. It had been called by the Pope. It had been officially opened by him at Bogota, at the end of the International Eucharistic Congress. And when the assembly moved from Bogota to Medellín three personal representatives of the Holy Father remained with us. We delegates had either been elected by our episcopal conferences, or we had been nominated by the Pope. All of the resolutions had been freely discussed and passed by vote. Every word and sentence of the document had been examined in Rome. Everything had been approved. Even our denunciation of internal colonialism, in other words the colonialism that is practised within our country and our continent by privileged groups who maintain their wealth by keeping their compatriots in misery and poverty. Even our denunciation of stratified injustice, in other words injustice that arises not just occasionally or accidentally, but structurally, and can only be abolished by changing social structures. Even our decision not just to preach the ideal of education as a liberating force, but to put it into practice. All of this was there, in the official documents produced by the conference, for everyone to read; and young people read them.

But we didn't have the right to be naive. We were grown men, bishops, ministers. We had experts with us, highly-qualified advisers. We knew that the privileged classes couldn't listen to all of this without reacting. A reaction was inevitable, obvious. It was bound to come.

And when it came it was intelligently done. The privileged classes are very reluctant to attack the Church. They have enormous respect for the Pope. They are loyal to the true Church and are the true, the only defenders of Christian civilization. And it was love of the Church, simply love of the Church, that prompted them to denounce the Marxist infiltration that was gnawing at its heart... Because clearly all this talk of oppressors and oppressed was Marxist-inspired; the idea of denouncing internal colonialism could only have come from Moscow; the desire to put an end to stratified injustice is nothing but Maoism. Clearly!

How can I explain it? ... It's true that the Church has always been a friend and ally to the rich. On the great *fazendas* [plantations] in Brazil there was always a church and a padre. And now suddenly the Church had become a problem. But no, it wasn't possible. It couldn't be the Church: it must be something else. It must be Marxist infiltration among the students, among the nuns and the priests, and even among the bishops! ...

On one occasion – after 1964, I'm not sure exactly when – a delegation of women came to see the Papal Nuncio, Monsignor Lombardi. They had come to present him with a list of bishops tainted with Marxism, whom they wanted him to transfer or even dismiss entirely. They began to read the names on the list. But after the first name Monsignor Lombardi – he was a very fine Nuncio – stopped them. 'Forgive me, ladies. Don't you think you have said enough? I can't listen to you any more. The first name is enough to tell me that I needn't know any more. Please excuse me.'

Nevertheless some members of the hierarchy believed – and there are some who still believe today – that the Church really was being infiltrated by Marxists. And they expelled the Catholic University Youth movement from Catholic Action ...

The reason why Catholic University Youth became radical and why it founded *Acão Popular* [Popular Action], was that it believed the social encyclicals were not meant to remain on paper. The crime these young people committed was to believe that the decisions of the Second Vatican Council were not meant to remain on paper! So you see in the beginning we bishops were directly responsible for this radicalization among the youth movements – in University Youth, the students' movement, as well as the Independent Youth movement and Young Workers. And we didn't even understand that! ... Things are different now. As more and more priests and nuns and bishops – and their numbers are growing, thank God – become determined to put the brave resolutions of the modern Church into practice, more and more young people are coming back with renewed confidence and trust.

It seems as if Catholic Action in Brazil is like a page that is turned, as if you have somehow gone beyond it now, and see the future of the apostolate of the laity in terms very different from Catholic Action. People say that Catholic Action was an élitist movement, that it was an emanation from 'above' rather than an expression from below. With the grass roots, and the apostolate of the people . . .

We are enormously grateful to Catholic Action. It was our seminary, our noviciate. It trained some of our best militants. It prepared the way for the Council. But of course after the Council it was no longer simply a matter of allowing the laity the right, the honour, the glory of participating in hierarchical apostolate! The Council had recognized the specific and essential role of the laity. The layman is no longer defined negatively: he's no longer 'one who is not a member of the clergy'. He has his own role and his own positive definition.

You mentioned the grass roots communities: they really are a great blessing. They have enormous potential.

At one time I believed that institutions could be converted: I mean universities, trade unions, big organizations, the press . . . But that was an impossible dream. Today I realize that the ways of the Lord are not exactly our ways. My hope lies now in the grass roots communities.

Think of a parish priest. He's probably quite happy because he holds six, seven, eight masses on a Sunday and his church is full every time. But you know very well that the people who come to mass, particularly in the cities – even in Rome! – represent only a small percentage of the population. And what about the others? All the people who don't come to church? They're living their own lives in their own neighbourhoods, their own natural communities. So now we've begun to approach these communities. Nuns and priests, and above all lay workers, are trying to live and work among them, are trying to help people to identify their problems and organize themselves to solve them. We say to these men and women who wish to work for human advancement: 'Don't think that the government is going to come here and solve your problems for you! You've got to think for yourselves, act for yourselves. Later perhaps, when the government sees you all united, it may come and help.' And it's the same with the Church. We can't expect everything to be thought of and arranged and decided from without, by the powers that be, on behalf of everyone. We must imitate Christ. Christ came for everybody, for all people of all countries and all times. But nevertheless He became incarnate among one race, in one society. He adopted a language and customs that were not the language and customs of all people of all countries and all times. He was the son of a Nazareth carpenter. We need to understand this lesson of incarnation: we must each remain bound to humanity as a whole, and to the universal Church, but at the same time become incarnate in our own particular Nazareth.

I think it's really impossible now to bring about changes from the top, from the *coupole*, as we say in Portuguese. The real changes will come from below. So yes, it's true that the grass roots communities are quite different from Catholic Action. But Catholic Action prepared the way.

> So you speak of Catholic Action as something in the past...?

Well, a past that was indispensable... But nowadays no layman is concerned merely with 'participating' in the hierarchical apostolate. The laity knows that it is the Church. Of course there are still some priests, and even some bishops, who don't entirely accept it; but gradually, little by little, we're moving forward and making progress. The grass roots communities are revealing new possibilities and teaching us new lessons.

For example, for a long time we had a rather ill-considered, negative attitude towards what we called 'popular religiosity'. We saw it as being riddled with superstition, even magic. Consequently it was considered a vital objective of pastoral work to abolish all traditional processions and ceremonies. But today we are beginning to understand the words of Christ: 'I thank Thee, O Father, because Thou hast hidden Thy truths from the great and the wise and the powerful, and Thou hast revealed them to the humble.' Now we have the people's evangelical movement known as The

Brothers' Meeting. There are some people in the groups who are educated, who have been to university; but many more who are illiterate, or semi-illiterate. Someone reads an extract from the Gospel, and then they all talk about it. And it's extraordinary how often the most profound, the most relevant comments come from the poorest and simplest people.

   Is that a local movement in Recife, or a national one?

There are all sorts of movements now with all sorts of different names, but the same inspiration. We are all doing our best to obey the promptings of the Holy Spirit. And you know the Holy Spirit doesn't have to wait for missionaries and bishops to transmit its message; it doesn't stop to choose the places where there are Catholics. They are everywhere, potentially: all men are the sons of God, united through Christ. So the Holy Spirit breathes; and very often when the missionaries arrive they are really surprised to find that the Holy Spirit has got there first!

It makes for some curious mixtures. We see it particularly in Brazil. We have many Africans in our country. We Christians imported slaves from Africa. They were brought here under appalling conditions. Even cattle were not transported like that. When they got here they were split up so that they wouldn't form groups: husbands separated from wives, children from parents. It was horrible! And as a recompense, as a first benefit of civilization, a first token of human and Christian advancement, they were baptized. Without any preparation, of course. That wasn't necessary: the baptism was enough in itself, wasn't it? All you needed was some water and the right words ... Nowadays we try to convert people before we baptize them. But in those days, when these poor creatures, these children of God, were oppressed and overburdened by our good intentions, I think the Holy Spirit protected them by letting them associate the names of our saints with their own gods and spirits ...

For instance, they often confuse the Virgin Mary with Iemanja. Iemanja is the goddess of the sea. She is greatly honoured in Brazil. And on the eighth of December, when I see the enormous crowds that gather to celebrate the Immaculate Conception, I'm convinced that two-thirds of the people are probably thinking of Iemanja. It's a real mixture of African religion and Christianity: they are there to honour the Blessed Virgin: they love the Mother of God, the Mother of Christ, sincerely; but they confuse Her somewhat with the goddess of the sea.

When you're here in my house you often hear someone knocking at the front door and shouting: 'Dom Helda! . . . Dom Hebe! . . .' All sorts of different names. It isn't the people's fault that my name is rather difficult to remember and pronounce! 'Helder' is really quite difficult! But imagine if I were to open the door and say: 'You've come to the wrong house. There's no one here called Dom Helda, or Dom Hebe! . . .' People don't need to pronounce my name impeccably for me to know that it's me they're calling, it's me they're looking for. It's the same with the Mother of God, who is also the Mother of Men, and the Mother of Fishermen: it really doesn't matter if people confuse Her name with that of Iemanja! . . .

> But are you not afraid that in respecting popular religiosity like this you may be cultivating 'the opium of the people'? People must have religion in the same way that they must have their festivals, their football or their samba, because they like it and need it . . .

You know, you have to start from where the people are. Imagine if I were to arrive among a tribe of Indians and say: 'Right! Now we're going to speak Portuguese. Because Portuguese is a real language, rich in history and culture. I don't need to learn the poor language of the Indians. Only Portuguese.' It's impossible. Incarnation means putting yourself on the level of the people you live and work with. Not so that you can stay there, of course, but so you can help them rise above it. The only way to help them rise is to start from where they are.

Look, here's a little book: *Cantigas do povo* [*Songs of the*

People]. It's a collection of folk songs put together by the Rural Evangelical Movement. I often base my morning radio programmes on these songs of the people. They're very powerful. Listen to this, for instance:

> I am the Christ, I am a North-Easterner
> A Sertanejo, worker, fighter for my cause . . .

The people already understand that we have no right to blame God for the problems that we have created ourselves. As if the Lord were responsible for the floods or the droughts! No! It would have been very easy for our Father to create a universe that was already perfect. But it would have been terribly boring for us to come into a world where everything had already been done, and done well, where everything was complete. So the Lord merely began the creative process, and entrusted man with the task of completing it. It is up to us to control the rivers. It's a question of intelligence and integrity. If we had shown sufficient intelligence and integrity in the past the droughts and the floods would already have been controlled. Nowadays deserts are being watered and rivers diverted. It's our own problem, not the Lord's:

> *A seca a cheia que nos vem de vez em quando*
> *Nao e castigo do Bom Deus vou lhe dizer*
> *Ele nos deixa tao somente como exemplo*
> *O que se pode mas se deixa de fazer . . .*

> *The droughts and the floods that afflict us sometimes*
> *Are not the good Lord's punishment, I tell you:*
> *They come to remind us, now as always*
> *Of the things that we could do, but leave undone . . .*

You say that this collection of songs is an expression of the people; but in fact it's an expression of the Rural Evangelical Movement – a small and particularly enlightened section of the population. Surely the vast majority of the people has been brought up to think in terms of praying for rain? ...

Yes, yes, you're right. For a long time we preached a very passive sort of religion: 'We must all have patience, be obedient, resign ourselves. We must accept suffering in this life in union with the suffering of Christ.' And a religion that called on magic. If there was a drought, we would organize a procession to pray for rain. And if too much rain fell, we'd have another procession . . . It's true. But these things I am talking about, these folk songs, are very widely known; they are the first results of evangelization.

Listen to this one. It's full of feeling: *Deus nao quer isso nao.* That's the refrain: 'No, God does not want that.' What God doesn't want is a world torn between an excess of money and mortal hunger, between loveless pleasures and appalling suffering, between soaring palaces and tumble-down shacks, between those who give orders and those who bend the knee. They're very simple words, very rhythmic. *Deus nao quer isso nao*: 'No, God does not want that.'

And listen to this song from the *sertão*:

> I am a simple peasant
> I make a living with my spade
> The harvest I gather
> Is shared with men who sow no seed
>
> But planting for sharing
> I won't do it any more!
>
> If it goes on any longer
> I will leave my *sertão*
> Though my eyes may fill with tears;
> And with sorrow in my heart
> I'll go to Rio and carry mortar
> For a builder's mason.
> Though the Lord may come and help us
> And send rain on the *sertão*.
>
> But planting for sharing
> I won't do it any more!

You're right when you say that all this is an expression of the Rural Evangelical Movement. But fatalism was also the expression of evangelization. We must be thankful that with the Lord's help we are beginning to change people's way of thinking and change their attitudes. But you have to start from where the people are. If I were to begin by abolishing all processions – or if I decided, for example, not to baptize children any longer because I can't evangelize them – I wouldn't get very far. It has to be a gradual process, this helping the people forward.

> I thought there had been a reaction against sacramentalism in the Brazilian Church – against the automatic dispensation of the sacraments?

That's also true. We've discovered that each sacrament calls for a period of preparation. We have to make it clear, for example, that baptism isn't simply an excuse to have a party, or to please your friends by asking them to be godfathers or godmothers. In the grass roots communities baptisms are very important and splendid: the baptism service is really the official introduction of a new member into the community. It isn't only the parents and the family who prepare for a baptism, but the whole community. It's the same with marriages.

> You speak for five minutes every morning on Radio Olinda. But for more than fifteen years, while you were in Rio de Janeiro, you had a great deal more exposure on radio and on television. Were you saying the same things then as you say now?

In Rio de Janeiro I had tremendous scope. I had a weekly television programme, and a daily radio programme – *Our Daily Bread* – on Radio Globo, which was the most important station in Brazil. I was often invited to appear on other programmes. In those days I was always trying to convey a little Christian message based on the events of daily life. My main concern was to show that with the help of the Lord anyone, no matter who or where he was, could open his eyes and ears and escape from his own egoism, and meet other people, all other people, instead of not listening to and not loving anyone but himself. That was my whole purpose:

helping people to see, to listen, to love ...

By the time I came here, to Recife, I was older and wiser. All sorts of things had happened – not just in Brazil and Latin America, but in the rest of the world. And I was coming home to my own people: I was born not far from here, in Ceará. All of which meant that I could perhaps see things more clearly and profoundly ...

As you know I'm no longer allowed to appear on television. And I can't speak on the radio either – only on Radio Olinda, which used to belong to this diocese and now belongs to the Paulinian Fathers.

I'm allowed one programme a week for preaching the Gospel. At present [1976] we have a whole hour for preaching to the people after mass. There is a whole team of people who prepare the programme and listeners are invited to come and discuss the Gospel and pray with us.

I also have a five-minute programme on Radio Olinda every day except Sunday. It's extremely well-placed: just after a football programme and just before the national news! So I make the most of it ... I often talk about one of these 'Songs of the People', for example. You have to know what the people are singing ... 'Listen to the voice of thy people'.

IN TOUCH WITH ROME

> 1950 was a Holy Year, and you organized a pilgrimage to Rome. It's remembered as something of an epic adventure: what was so special about it?

Yes, 1950, the Holy Year ... Well, there was a meeting one day at the Saint Joachim Palace, the archbishop's palace in Rio de Janeiro. Cardinal de Barros Camara needed someone to be secretary-general for the Holy Year in Brazil. He appointed me. So I had to organize various pilgrimages and celebrations all over the country.

At that time we could get from the government more or less anything we wanted. So we asked for a boat, and we were given a naval vessel, a troopship! Of course it wasn't terribly comfortable – it wasn't exactly a liner! ... I was told that it could hold no more than eight hundred people comfortably. The boat was delivered and the rest was up to us. There was a captain on board, and a full crew; but we had to organize things like food and accommodation.

I was in touch with the secretaries of all the dioceses, and we arranged that the boat would leave from Rio de Janeiro and call at Salvador de Bahia and Recife before heading for Europe. We were able to charge a ridiculously low fare.

But twenty-five days before we were due to leave we still had only two hundred and fifty passengers. So whenever anyone telephoned or cabled to ask if there was still room on board I would say yes. And during those last twenty-five days the number of passengers rose from two hundred and fifty to thirteen hundred and fifty ... I ought to have drawn the line at eight hundred: but I couldn't do it. You see for all these people it was their one opportunity in a lifetime of going to Europe and Rome: and when they had made up their minds to go they had already, spiritually, embarked. So it was impossible for me, spiritually, to refuse them this unique opportunity ...

When we left Rio de Janeiro there were already more than eight hundred people on board. It was dreadful. The conditions on a troopship are bad in any case. So a lot of people started complaining and saying: 'We don't want the boat to stop at Salvador or Recife. We won't allow it. We should head straight for Europe.'

I summoned all the pilgrims to a meeting on deck. There were no chairs or benches, but everyone was there. And I preached to them:

'Friends! We must recognize God's signs! All of us were prepared for a so-called pilgrimage: in fact we were thinking more in terms of an expedition, perhaps even a holiday. Now we must take advantage of the grace of God. Because it is the grace of God that has granted us this opportunity. We must seize it with both hands! We must transform our expedition, or our holiday, into a real pilgrimage, into something fine and hard. The crossing will take twenty-two days. It will require many sacrifices: there are no comfortable beds and very little food. Can you think of a better way of spending a Holy Year? This pilgrimage may change your life, your destiny, your eternity!

'So I'm going to make a suggestion. We shall call at Salvador and Recife. Anyone who wants to leave the ship will be perfectly free to do so and his fare will be refunded. But as for the rest, all those who choose to remain on board, I ask you, I beg you, to be ready and determined to welcome the newcomers aboard with open arms, like brothers. There are five hundred more pilgrims to come.'

Well, no one left the ship at Salvador. Everyone agreed to undertake the pilgrimage as the Lord had suggested. We got ourselves organized: we set up a whole system of spiritual activities and nourishment. Everyone felt that that first meeting on the deck between Rio de Janeiro and Salvador had been very important, and we decided to meet like that regularly. Some people were in charge of the singing while others were in charge of entertainments . . .

In those days one of my cardinal's major preoccupations was preventing women and girls from wearing trousers like men. He had issued a regulation: the wearing of trousers by women was absolutely forbidden. It was most important!

Well, soon after we set off several people became seasick. I mobilized all the passengers who were capable of helping: for instance, I said: 'I need as many nurses as possible.' And several young women came forward to help. And then: 'I need more volunteers to help look after the people who are ill, and the old people.' And more people came forward.

Since it was a troopship there were no staircases, between decks, but there were ladders, which were practically vertical. I remember on one occasion I got to the foot of one of these ladders and was about to go up when I saw there was a young nurse at the top, coming down with tea for the invalids. And suddenly the wind whipped up her skirts! She called to me: 'You see why we need trousers, Dom Helder!' Well, I trusted my cardinal. I knew I was entitled to modify his regulations. So after that I not only authorized, I recommended the wearing of trousers! . . .

I remember something else that happened soon after that first decisive sermon. Five women came to see me and said: 'Padre Helder, we are prostitutes. We live in the slums on the outskirts of Rio. We came, like everyone else, because we didn't want to miss the chance of going to Europe – to Paris, most of all. And we thought we could earn some money on the way. You can always find clients on a boat. But now we've come to tell you that you needn't worry about us. We know you aren't the kind of man who would punish us . . . But we listened to what you said. So don't worry: we won't work – not at any price – during the pilgrimage.'

And you know four of those women became my friends. One of them was even converted. The others went back to being prostitutes because there was nothing else they could do. But they all did their best to be good pilgrims . . . You see the Lord very often has surprises in store for us. Our ways are not the ways of the Lord . . .

Was this the first time you had left Brazil?

Yes, the first time. Of course, in order to preserve my moral strength and authority I always had to choose the most uncomfortable places to sit or sleep. I really had to do gymnastics to get into the corner where I slept. I benefited from the pilgrimage too ...

We landed at Naples and went by coach to Rome. Unfortunately I wasn't able to go back with the other pilgrims in our warship, because the cardinal wanted me back more quickly; so I flew back to Brazil.

The world secretary for the Holy Year was Monsignor Pignedoli. Monsignor Pignedoli invited me back to Rome at the end of 1950 for a meeting of all the national secretaries. The first World Conference of the Laity was being held at the same time, and I was asked to prepare the Brazilian contribution to the conference. The programme covered a number of different themes, and we prepared a paper on each one. But I remember each paper ended with the same conclusion: 'None of this will be possible or effective until there is a national conference of bishops in Brazil.'

The Papal Nuncio in Brazil, Monsignor Chiarlo, felt I should take advantage of this visit to Rome to present the Vatican officially with the idea of a national conference of bishops. He had arranged a meeting for me with Monsignor Montini, who was then at the Secretariat of State at the Vatican. But the Lord conducted the meeting in a very strange way ...

When I arrived in Rome I went straight to the Vatican with the diplomatic bag that had been entrusted to me and confirmed the request that I had made by letter for an audience with Monsignor Montini. I was sure that the audience would be granted almost immediately.

I was staying in one of the many temporary lodging houses that had opened up around the Vatican during the Holy Year. I remember there was no heating, and it was the middle of winter. So I waited. Days went by and I heard nothing from the Vatican. And I waited. But finally I got a message: 'Monsignor Montini will receive you at the Vatican on 21 December at 1 p.m.' I was very glad, because

I saw the great day approaching for the Brazilian conference of bishops.

When I got up during the night of 20 December for the
vigil that I wanted to dedicate to preparing myself for the
audience, I noticed something dripping from my ears. It was
blood. And later, when two young Brazilian seminarists
joined me for mass, I realized I couldn't hear anything. Not a
thing! Well! I was already worried about how I was going
to express myself to Monsignor Montini in my poor French –
which was a great deal worse in those days than it is today.
And now I wouldn't be able to hear him either! All through
mass I was completely deaf. And the audience was at one
o'clock in the afternoon . . .

So I put myself in the hands of the Lord. I asked my
guardian angel to protect me. I should explain that although
I have every respect for theologians and their arguments,
nothing they say can alter my simple, childlike devotion to
my guardian angel. I can't possibly doubt him: I should be
not only ungrateful, but blind, if I did. Since I don't know
his real name for the time being, I call him José. That's
what my mother used to call me when she was pleased with
me, particularly if she saw that I had done something well
and no one else had appreciated it. 'Have courage, José!'
she used to say. So it's the name I love best, and I've given it
to my guardian angel.

'Can we come to an agreement about this, José?' I said.
'If this idea of a national conference of bishops is simply my
idea and nothing else, it's very easy for you to make sure
that I can't hear anything and can't make myself understood.
But if it is the Lord's plan, then I ask you to help me and
protect me, which is also very easy for you to do: and I will
need to be able to hear and talk. Is that agreed? Then let's go!'

When I went in to see Monsignor Montini I was perfectly calm, utterly at ease . . . And José did a wonderful job!
I could hear normally, and I even managed to say what I
wanted to in French. Everything was fine.

I discovered that the reason Monsignor Montini had de-
layed the interview was so that he could study in advance all
the documents on the apostolate of the laity that I had
brought in the diplomatic bag – all the documents that con-

cluded by saying a national conference of bishops was essential. He could read Portuguese without difficulty.

It's strange how diplomats always retain their sense of diplomacy...At one point, after we had been talking for about half an hour, Monsignor Montini decided to test me. Or at least that was how I interpreted his question: 'Monsignor, I am convinced now of the necessity, in fact the urgency, of setting up a Brazilian national conference of bishops. But one thing still troubles me. This is a conference of bishops. But from everything I have read, everything I have heard and everything I know, the secretary of this conference of bishops has to be you, Padre Helder Camara. No one else could do it. You are the natural choice for the position. But you are not a bishop...'

You see he wanted to find out if there was some ulterior motive behind my plan: if I was trying to put myself forward as a candidate for the episcopate...So I replied: 'Forgive me, Monsignor Montini, but you of all people should not be concerned about that. Because unless I'm wrong you yourself are not a bishop, and yet in your work at the Secretariat of State the Lord uses you, in the service of the Holy Father, as a link between all the bishops in the world. So why should I not serve Christ and His Church by acting as a link between a small group of bishops in a little corner of the world – without being a bishop myself?' Monsignor Montini smiled. After that we were friends.

> What had made you think that a national conference of bishops was suddenly so necessary, so urgent?

Until the beginning of this century there was a very small number of dioceses in Brazil. And then in a matter of a few years the Holy See decided to increase the number of dioceses and bishops. Now when a priest is appointed bishop and entrusted with a diocese he immediately comes up against all sorts of different and complex problems. He hasn't time to come to Rio de Janeiro: the country is too vast, the distances too great. He has no one to help him. When I thought of a national conference, I envisaged a national secretariat as well which would serve all the bishops of the Church of Christ Incarnate in this land of Brazil.

So you won your case, and were cured of your deafness at the same time ...

No, when I came out of the Vatican I was deaf again ... People had to speak to me in sign language, or the Brazilian seminarist who was looking after me would write me little notes. I had to get back to Brazil. But I was taken to a hospital in Rome run by priests, and the doctors said I shouldn't travel. I argued with them: 'But aeroplanes are pressurized!' And they said: 'You might lose your hearing permanently.' But I flew back to Brazil all the same.

And you aren't deaf. Did you ever find out what had happened to your ears?

I think it was an incipient rupture of the ear-drum. But it got better.

And so you began to set up the conference of bishops?

Not immediately. We waited a whole year for the official response from Rome, and we didn't hear a word. So I took advantage of the next opportunity of going back to see Monsignor Montini. 'I owe you an apology,' he said. 'But I promise that the conference of Brazilian bishops will be created within two months.' And so it was. Cardinal Motta of São Paulo was elected the first president, and I was appointed secretary-general, which I remained from 1952 to 1964, when the Holy Father entrusted me with the diocese of Olinda and Recife.

I took it upon myself to make another suggestion to Monsignor Montini at the same time: 'Your Excellency, it will be more difficult in Brazil than in any other Latin American country for a national episcopal conference to succeed, because it is the biggest country, with the most dioceses and bishops, and conditions vary enormously from one region to another. But if our experiment works, perhaps we could think of setting up a continental conference, with a secretariat to serve all the bishops of Latin America?'

A few years later we were making preparations for the International Eucharistic Congress in Rio de Janeiro. Reports were sent to Monsignor Montini in Rome, and he could see that everything was going quite well. So then he sent us a letter which took us by surprise: 'Are your preparations for the Eucharistic Congress sufficiently advanced that we could think of convoking an assembly of Latin American bishops in Rio de Janeiro at the end of the Congress, as a sequel to the Congress, which could form the basis of a Latin American episcopal conference?' I was delighted: it was our dream come true.

I handed over to my brother, Dom Távora, the task of finalizing preparations for the Eucharistic Congress, and devoted myself to organizing the assembly of Latin American bishops which gave birth to the Latin American Episcopal Council, CELAM.

There was another occasion, still during the reign of Pius XII, when I took the opportunity of going to Rome to put forward an idea. I saw Montini first of course, but then I was able to speak directly to the Pope. 'Holy Father, may I make a suggestion? As you know all the Americas – North America, Central America and South America – share common problems. So if you were to approve a small meeting – which I envisage taking place in Washington – between six bishops from the United States, six from Canada, and six from Latin America . . . And please let me make it absolutely clear that we Latin American bishops would have no intention whatsoever of asking the other countries for money or priests. It would simply be an opportunity to begin studying together the problems we all share. Because in Latin America we have problems that can never be solved without the understanding and active collaboration of our brothers in North America. We have to make sure that American and Canadian bishops find the courage to recognize the injustices that are oppressing the Latin American continent, and mobilize the spiritual force that the Church represents in North America.'

Pius XII understood and accepted the idea immediately: 'As far as I am concerned, I think it is an admirable idea. But would you be good enough to discuss it with Monsignor Tardini and Monsignor Montini as well? If they both agree, then you may go ahead.' And they did agree.

So you put your plan into action?

Yes, but as soon as the bishops in the United States heard about it they thought we were going to ask them for money. They wrote and said so to the Secretariat of State at the Vatican. The Vatican sent me a copy of the letter and asked me to reply. So I wrote back to them: 'No, absolutely not! That isn't what we want. What we want is your understanding; we want the opportunity to study together the problems that are not just Latin American problems, but the problems of all the Americas!'

The meeting took place. I was there as was the great Dom Manuel Larrain, Bishop of Talca, in Chile; or rather, he particularly was there. But at the end of the meeting something terrible happened.

The Holy See had sent a representative to the meeting. And this representative said to the United States bishops: 'I am here in your country as an apostolic delegate. I know you quite well. I know that you like practical, concrete things. So let us conclude these three days of discussion like this: for the next ten years, one million dollars a year shall go to Latin America, and ten per cent of priests, nuns and lay workers.' I tried to protest: 'Please, Your Excellency! That is not at all in the spirit of this meeting!'

Did your links with the North American Church end there?

The important thing to see and bear in mind is the gradual change that has come about in the attitudes of the United States and Canadian Church hierarchies. It would be ridiculous to attribute that change to the influence of this or that individual. It is solely the work of the Holy Spirit.

You have to understand that in the United States, for a long time after Independence, the Roman Catholic Church was considered suspect and somehow un-American. Some churches and convents were even burned down. For a long time American Catholics devoted most of their energy to developing their own community, their parishes and their schools. Beyond that they were very diffident. I remember once, when John Fitzgerald Kennedy became a candidate for the Presidency, I said to an American bishop: 'So you have a Catholic candidate.' And he said: 'Yes, but he isn't really one of our boys, because he didn't go to one of our schools.' In other words only people who went to Catholic schools were considered true Catholics! . . .

But now, it's a miracle! Take for instance the way in which the North American Church saw its role in the celebration of the Bicentenary. During 1975 the bishops organized six regional congresses, culminating in a great national congress in 1976. The theme of these congresses was taken from the Pledge of Allegiance that American soldiers make when they promise to fight so that everyone may live in justice and liberty: 'Liberty and justice for all.'

At congress after congress bishops, priests, nuns and above all members of the laity – and not just Catholics – called on the whole nation to open its eyes and ask itself the questions: 'You remember our fine motto: "Liberty and justice for all"? Do you feel that you are free in this country? Do you think there is justice here for yourself, for your family, for your fellow workers or students, for your community? Do liberty and justice really exist here? Even for blacks? Even for Mexicans? Even for Puerto Ricans? Even for Chinese? And do you think the United States helps to promote liberty and justice in the rest of the world?'

That's the kind of awareness we dream of! And I can assure you, because I know, it takes a great deal of courage to commit yourself to the task of making people aware.

Which reminds me of a conversation I once had with my brother Fulton Sheen when he was auxiliary bishop of New York. He had become a television personality and he came to Rio de Janeiro for three days when he was at the height of his fame. I stayed with him all the time he was here; I went everywhere with him. We were very close friends.

On the last day, just before he was leaving, I said to him:

'Do you mind if I ask you something? After spending these three days with you I know that we have a great deal in common, we share the same attitudes to the world and the Church. Why don't you take advantage of your reputation, and of television, which can work miracles, and campaign against, say, racism? Why don't you make use of the power you have at your disposal and denounce, for example, the injustices of the international politics of commerce? Why do you associate yourself with attitudes that neither of us agrees with?'

And he answered: 'My brother, I am glad that you had the courage and the confidence in me to ask that question. You might have gone on wondering without saying anything to me. But I can explain it very simply. As you know the bishops of the United States donate one million dollars a year to Latin America. Thanks to television, I'm also able to raise eighty million dollars a year for the Holy Father's *Propaganda Fide*. This money enables the Pope to help schools, leper hospitals and general hospitals all over the world. Now I assure you that if I were to go on television tomorrow and denounce racism or the injustice of the international politics of commerce this money would immediately stop coming in. So it is a choice that I have had to make. I prefer to be considered weak or naive or unprincipled. I'm quite aware that that is how I appear; and I accept it. Someone has to sacrifice himself for the sake of the emergency work, while others work towards structural change. I am glad that my brother Dom Helder speaks the truths that I am not able to speak. In a way, you see, we are complementary.'

After that I kissed his hands. I was very moved: 'So you accept . . . That is true poverty, to accept being judged naive, bourgeois, blind to injustice. And you have chosen it deliberately.' I kissed his hands.

When you are working for human advancement you discover that there are – and no doubt always will be – some people who cannot really benefit from that advancement. Something – whether it's old age, ill health, or the consequences of malnutrition – holds them back and leaves them by the wayside. Perhaps I could draw a military analogy – although as you know I hate war! An army decides to capture a town, and marches towards it. The troops must not forget for one moment that their objective is to defeat and take possession of the town. But if along the way they come across people who are wounded and can't fight, and who may die if they are not cared for; and if the troops can help them, carry them on their shoulders, or take them to a hospital, without losing sight of their own objective – then they must do it. I often think that in the war against injustice eighty per cent of our time and efforts must be devoted to changing structures and promoting human advancement; but twenty per cent must be set aside for tending the wounded and the victims of the war ...

12

HOLY FATHER, FORGIVE ME . . .

> During all the time that you were secretary of the conference of Brazilian bishops, and afterwards as well, you had a great deal to do with Papal Nunciates, the Curia, and with the Pope himself. I remember how attentively you read and annotated Jean Guitton's *Dialogues with Paul VI*: it was as if you yourself were engaged in an intimate conversation with the Pope . . .

Dialogues with Paul VI is one of Jean Guitton's most successful books. Are they real or imaginary dialogues? When did the Holy Father really say these things? When did his friend interpret his silences? . . . Nevertheless Paul VI recognized himself in the dialogues.

All I can venture to do is tell you the things that I said to the Holy Father, whether in person or in thought, from a distance, from my heart.

On one occasion, when I was returning from the World Meeting of Religions for Justice and Peace in Kyoto, I had the opportunity of speaking – in person or in a dream? I don't know – to Pope Paul. 'You know, Holy Father, all the religions represented in Kyoto were obliged to be humble. Every religion preaches a message that should at least make men more human. So as long as the world remains so inhuman no religion can presume to be proud.

'But our position, Holy Father, the position of Christianity, was the least tenable of all. Because we must not forget that

the privileged people throughout Latin America who maintain their wealth by keeping their fellow citizens in misery
are all – at least in name and origin – Christians. And we
must not forget that the rich countries in the world, the
countries that are constantly becoming richer, and who
maintain their wealth by keeping poor countries in misery
are all – at least in name and origin – Christian. What have
we done with the Gospel?

'So I should like to suggest some things you could do,
Holy Father – because words are no longer sufficient
nowadays, only actions will do, and not just symbolic
actions, but a whole life. But I warn you that you won't be
able to put these suggestions into practice by yourself. First
you have to create circumstances in which it will be possible
for you to act.' And then I put forward my suggestions.

'I saw for myself at Kyoto that all the major religions are
caught up in the mesh of Capitalism. But they haven't all
been so foolhardy as to ally themselves with banks! Oh,
Holy Father, if only you could close the Bank of the Holy
Spirit at least! But I realize you can't do it yet.

'Another request, Holy Father. You are a logical man. You
realized and understood at once that the Pope is not a king,
and you have never, never worn the tiara since you re-
nounced it solemnly and absolutely. But then why, Holy
Father, do you preserve the ambiguity of all these ambassadors around you? And why do you still keep your
nuncios all over the world? I realize that for the time being
you can't change anything by yourself. But if only one day,
during some fine Christmas mass, you could bid farewell to
their excellencies the ambassadors, and recall your nuncios
to Rome . . . Power and authority must be shared equally
among the bishops: episcopal collegiality must be our aim!'

I know that there are times and places where bishops
alone – even joined in an episcopal college – are helpless.
There are situations where nuncios are indispensable –
particularly in countries where the Church is not free. But I
told the Pope that this did not necessitate maintaining
nuncios permanently all over the world; that nuncios were
not always well-equipped to carry out the very delicate
missions that they were often entrusted with; and that per-

haps instead a group of experts – even laymen – might be sent to help in a situation where the local hierarchy was unable to assume full responsibility alone . . . And I concluded with another suggestion:

'As you know, Holy Father, rightly or wrongly, the Vatican has become a negative sign that alienates many people, particularly the young. You know Rome like the back of your hand: if only you could find yourself a little house on some little square, and live there instead . . . Then you could really meet all the people who come to Rome: you would be among them, instead of seeing them only from a great height and distance, as you do when you speak to them from your balcony. Oh, Holy Father! I can't face any more of those dreadful public audiences in Saint Peter's Square on Sundays: they make you seem so far away . . . You must go out among the people! Of course some people would be afraid then that you might be killed, you might be assassinated. Forgive me, Holy Father, but I pray every night during every vigil, that the Pope may take this risk: it is such a long time since a shepherd died for his sheep.'

And the Pope smiled. He understood that there was no ulterior motive behind what I said: I did not mean to be presumptuous. I was simply expressing a profound conviction.

But I know the Pope cannot bring about the necessary changes by himself. I know that because I know I myself cannot always manage to bring about the changes I should like to see in my own little diocese in this remote corner of the world. I also have to rely on other people to help, and I am often defeated.

> So you knew that the wishes you were expressing to the Pope would remain merely pious hopes . . .

No. There were plans for helping the Pope: because no Pope can achieve anything by himself. One day – was it a dream or did it really happen? I don't know – one day I went to see a friend of mine who worked in the Curia in Rome, and I said to him: 'The Pope needs help.' I gave him a list of ten names, the names of ten distinguished people whom the

Pope had summoned to Rome to renew the Curia. I believed, I was convinced, that if these people worked closely together they could not only give one another mutual support, but also help the Pope to put the resolutions of the Council into action, and to bring about structural reforms in the Church which alone would give it the moral authority it needed to persuade the secular world to reform its own structures. Already, through the agency of the Pope, the Holy Spirit had introduced into the government of the Church at least ten very effective, competent and courageous people. The problem was that as soon as they got to Rome these people became enmeshed in the attitudes and procedures of the Curia.

I made a similar approach to the heads of the religious communities, and I said the same thing to all these influential men and women: 'It isn't a question of conspiring against the Pope! On the contrary! It's a question of establishing links between all the people in the Curia and the religious orders who want to help and support the Pope.'

That's my dream, a group of people like that . . . In reality what happens is that every day the Holy Father receives letters and reports that point out everything that's going wrong, all the dangers that are threatening and all the mistakes that have been made or are about to be made . . . And among all these letters and reports are all sorts of calumnies, lies and interpretations that are consciously or unconsciously distorted. Naturally all of this worries and distresses the Pope . . . What we need is a group of people who will help the Holy Father to see things clearly, who will support him, and make it possible for him to take action.

> And does this . . . lobby that you dreamed of now exist?

It's beginning to, it's beginning to . . . But I'm told it's very difficult and that the most effective and courageous people become . . . timid when they get to Rome. Well, you know, I myself can be timid, if it comes to that!

> I must say I wouldn't have thought you were timid . . .

I'll tell you a story. On one occasion, during the Vatican Council, when I was in the United States, I wanted to speak to Cardinal Mayer, the Archbishop of Chicago. He was kind enough to invite to dinner Dom Manuel Larrain and some other bishops and myself. The next day, just before I was due to leave Chicago, I decided to telephone the archbishop's secretary: 'I need to see the cardinal and talk to him.' 'But you saw him yesterday evening and dined with him!' 'I need to talk to the cardinal. I have something very important to say to him!' The cardinal agreed to see me. 'Your Eminence, I'm sorry I didn't find an opportunity of saying this to you yesterday evening. Don't you think that the American bishops ought to play a far more important part in the Council? With your help it could forge ahead. You know that whenever one of you speaks, people listen. But so far the American bishops have not exerted their influence in the Council; and it's because they have no leader. So what I want to say is: why don't you assume the role of leader?' And he replied: 'Do you think it's easy to be leader of the American bishops?' 'And do you think it's easy for a little Latin American bishop to speak like this to a great North American cardinal?' He smiled, and after that we became good friends.

Cardinal Mayer began preparing to take on the role that I had presumed to propose to him. But I didn't know that he was already very ill; and he died a short time after that.

> I'd like to come back if I may to the episcopal conferences. You were one of the prophets and pioneers of collegiality and are well aware of its advantages. But doesn't it also have many drawbacks? I'm thinking of all the bureaucracy, technocracy and perhaps even mediocrity that the work of secretariats, committees, experts and commissions may entail; while personal inspiration and charisma has to be submerged and diluted in an anonymous majority ...

Every majority is the expression of an active minority. In every human group, and therefore in episcopal conferences as well, the Holy Spirit moves a minority. If there is a problem, it is this minority that faces it. It has to be careful of two things.

First, it must not impose its point of view on the rest. It should explain its principles clearly; but at the same time it must make it clear that it has no wish to impose those principles on others. It needs to convince, not to vanquish.

Secondly, it must enact the principles it preaches, and enact them humbly. The active minority is no more intelligent, no more shrewd, no more human or no more holy than the rest. Pharisaism is a deadly temptation: without humility and without love . . .

But there are minorities at work, not in just one or two episcopal conferences, but in conferences all over the world, even in Rome. We have to understand what the Holy Spirit tells us through the Gospel and through the entire history of the Church up to the last Council. We need a minority in the Vatican that can understand and enact not only episcopal collegiality but also co-responsibility in the Church of the Lord; that can understand and enact the primacy of the Pope in terms of service and love, and only in terms of service and love: that is essential for ecumenism; that can understand and enact the Roman Curia not as a kind of super-state, but as an instrument to serve all of God's people, in other words to serve the whole of the Church, and not just the Pope and the hierarchy.

And it won't be long, it won't be long . . .

> When you say there is a minority in every episcopal conference working towards these ideals . . .

I mean it is the Holy Spirit who evokes the ideas and who does the work. There's no need to send messengers . . .

> Did you follow the argument that arose after the Council between the Dutch Church and Rome concerning the relationship between the 'centre' and the 'periphery', between 'unity', 'uniformity' and 'plurality'? Do you think these problems were universal, or were they confined to the Church in Holland?

They were universal, and very real, problems. Take for example the so-called Dutch catechism: it seems to me essential that a similar attempt to interpret the religion of all time should be made everywhere where the Church of Christ has been incarnated. Every local Church faces the problem of how to incarnate the unique and eternal Gospel in space and time. The Dutch bishops were endeavouring to present the doctrine of eternity to people of today. If similar efforts could be made in Africa, Asia and Latin America it would really be an enactment of the Second Vatican Council.

The things that are happening in Holland are happening to some extent in other places, too. When I go on lecture tours, I am always careful to ask in advance for the approval and consent of the local bishop in the place where I am supposed to speak. On one occasion I was invited to speak at a university in the diocese of a brother bishop who was reputed to be very conservative. He had already given me his formal consent; but about two hours before my lecture was due to start the bishop came to see me at the place where I was staying. He was very young and forceful, and he said straight away: 'I'm so glad I've found you here and have the chance to talk to you. Because I want to tell you that I totally disagree with your view of the world, and the way you are trying to reduce Christianity to humanism.' 'Monsignor, I am also very glad – that you have been so frank with me. I am sure that we can be friends, because if people are frank it is always possible to hold a dialogue. Tell me, did you read about my view of the world, and this humanism that you disapprove of, in a book, or in one of my lectures?' 'No, I've never read anything you have written.' 'Then perhaps you have heard me speak?' 'No, I've never heard you speak.' 'Well, then, Monsignor, let us make the most of the time at our disposal. I will tell you very simply how I regard the world and humanity, and how I see the role of the Church in the service of humanity. Afterwards you can tell me what you don't like. And since I am a guest in your diocese I will not mention any subject in my lecture on which we disagree.'

I gave a short summary of my attitudes and my way of thinking. And my brother bishop said: 'I agree with everything you've said.' 'Monsignor,' I replied, 'this is very serious. I am an old bishop, and you are a young bishop; you are just beginning your episcopal life. So allow me to say, as one brother to another, that this is very serious. I come here and you tell me that you disagree with my view of the world. Then you are frank enough to tell me that you are not really familiar with my philosophy, and that you have neither read nor heard a single word of it. Now I should like to ask you: have you read all the other works that you denounce?' And he answered: 'I can see that today is going to be a turning point in my life!'

We walked to the university together. The lecture hall was full of young people, and they burst into applause as we went in. The nuncio was already there. I was shown to my place between the other two. I gave my lecture, and then afterwards as usual I tried to answer questions.

Finally, when it was nearly midnight, a girl stood up and said: 'Dom Helder, I am sorry to have to ask you this question now, because it is embarrassing. We like you, and we don't like having to embarrass you. But do you know the two men who are beside you? Do you know what they are like?' And she went on to say some terrible things about my brother bishop and the papal nuncio. 'We're sorry to have to make things difficult for you, Dom Helder: we know you can't answer!'

But I took the microphone and said: 'I can answer, and I will! When you go out to speak to young people you have to have the courage to speak. Young people will accept the fact that you have different opinions from theirs, but they won't accept fear and lack of courage. So I will answer! I would remind you that the Church of Christ, which is divine by virtue of its Founder, nevertheless suffers from our human failings. So first I will tell you about the human failings of the sovereign pontiff, then the Roman Curia. From the Roman Curia I will go on to the nuncios, the bishops, the priests, and the nuns. And finally I will come to the human weakness of the laity. Oh, yes! Even you, especially you young ones, have a very grave responsibility!'

I summoned up all my courage and gave a brief account of the human failings of the Pope, the Curia, the nuncios, the bishops and the priests: so that in the end I was entitled to say some very severe, harsh things about the responsibilities of the laity. For example, I said: 'Very often it is you who are responsible for the positions that bishops and priests adopt: yet then you reproach them for maintaining those positions! Because you don't speak to them, you don't keep them informed, you don't tell them what the Holy Spirit has suggested to you. If a layman asks to see a bishop on his own in order to attack him brutally, he can have little hope of success. But if several people approach a bishop together, well-prepared and in a spirit of humility and love; and if the bishop sees that they have come not merely to criticize and argue but are motivated by a constructive love of the Church, then collaboration is possible. We are all the Church of Christ! We don't belong to the Church in order to destroy one another! Instead of you young people attacking my brother bishop or Monsignor the nuncio, and instead of Monsignor the nuncio and my brother bishop attacking you, let us recognize that we all have human failings, and that we are all brothers in Christ.'

Afterwards the nuncio said to me: 'The thing that strikes me most is the importance of being present. All through the evening I was thinking that I could have stayed at home. But then tomorrow someone would have come and given me an account of your speech: "Monsignor Helder attacked the Pope, the Roman Curia, the nuncios and the bishops . . ." But I was here, and I heard you myself. You gave the only answer that was possible under the circumstances.' The nuncio embraced me in silence, and then he added: 'Ask the Lord to make this a turning point in my life.'

I mention that incident in relation to the debate between Rome and the Church in Holland. There are misunderstandings, problems caused by misapprehensions, everywhere. We are all novices in the art of dialogue. It's very easy to talk about dialogue, but it's very hard actually to have a dialogue . . . To talk and know how to listen. To talk and know how to receive . . . Truth is so vast that each of us can see only one angle, one aspect of it. If only we could piece our little glimpses together, instead of fighting one another. But we're tills novices at that, and often rather inept novices...

13

THE EUCHARIST OF THE POOR

There is one year in particular that I should like to talk about: 1955. It was the year of the International Eucharistic Congress in Rio de Janeiro: a dazzling event which you were in charge of organizing. What strikes me most of all is the contrast between this and the other enterprise you had managed successfully five years earlier: for the Holy Year pilgrimage to Rome you relied on modest means, almost improvisation; for the Eucharistic Congress you had vast resources and put on a spectacular display. In retrospect, do you not feel that you were drifting into the 'triumphalism' that was later heavily criticized at the Council, and by yourself?

In those days I made a clear distinction between things that affected my humble self and things that served to glorify the Lord. I was following in the footsteps of our dear parish priest of Ars. I took exactly the same position as Jean-Marie Vianney: he was very severe, even austere, towards himself, but a spendthrift when it came to glorifying Christ.

I was familiar with the history of international eucharistic congresses; they had begun, in Lille, with this same idea. Since the Son of God had chosen to disappear, to hide Himself, reduce Himself apparently to a physical state, to make Himself totally dependent upon us men, I liked the idea of a congress where mankind could glorify Christ. It's true we already had the festival of Maundy

Thursday, and Corpus Christi – but nevertheless. It seemed to me perfectly normal, legitimate and indisputable that we should mobilize all possible resources to give glory to Christ. Even in a poor country. I had absolutely no doubts about it. I thought that celebrating the glory of the Lord would open people's eyes and touch their hearts.

Taking advantage of the Church's political influence in Brazil at the time, the president of the International Eucharistic Congress, Cardinal de Barros Camara, and I, the secretary-general of the Congress, went to see the President of the Republic. We explained to him briefly what a eucharistic congress is, and he immediately offered his support:

'But this is very important! People will come from all over the world! The first thing I must do is appoint Coelho de Lisboa as ambassador with the special responsibility and power to ensure that you get all the assistance you require from all the ministries and government departments. Have you any immediate requests?' 'Yes, Mister President, we would like to make one initial request. As you know the Congress will attract great crowds of people, but there is no open space in Rio de Janeiro large enough to hold such crowds.' 'So?' 'So we wondered . . . Of course couldn't do it by ourselves, but with your help . . . The government has a plan for filling in part of the bay and extending the land out into the sea. If only you could carry out this scheme in time for the Congress, it would be ideal. We could build an altar on it like a boat, with a sail, like a gigantic *jangada*.' 'The ambassador will put you in touch with the engineers and the work may begin at once!' It was like that.

But we had problems with the mayor of Rio de Janeiro, who put forward all sorts of objections and the work was held up. The cardinal asked me to go and see the President again:

'Mister President, the cardinal doesn't wish to press you, but it is time that is pressing on us. If the engineering work is held up any longer we won't have time to prepare the site for the Congress. And we shall have to inform the Holy Father.'

The president immediately rang to summon an aide: 'Send for Ambassador Coelho de Lisboa at once!' And when the ambassador arrived he said: 'Go and find the mayor, wherever he is. Today is Saturday. Tell him that work will begin at seven o'clock on Monday morning. The esplanade must be built!'

But then there was another problem. A very important lady who had connections with the directors of the major newspapers in Brazil had been planning to use this site to build a modern art museum. I tried to explain to her via my friend Santiago Dantas that she need only wait until after the Eucharistic Congress. 'After that the esplanade will be of no further use to us, and you can build your museum.' But she didn't believe us. It wasn't until after the Congress was over that she realized I had been telling the truth. The modern art museum is there now.

Organizing the International Eucharistic Congress represented a great challenge. It was the first time we had been responsible for an international enterprise on this scale. The cardinal came from Santa Catarina, and I, as you know, from Fortaleza in Ceará. But we had a whole team of remarkably devoted, generous and intelligent helpers. We had to think of everything. And afterwards everyone said that it went very very well.

Have you any idea what the Congress cost?

No, none at all. As I said, the money didn't matter because we were glorifying the Lord. But of course we did need money, and we thought of all sorts of ways of getting it. For example, when we published books it was very easy to add a note at the end saying that they had been published 'with the help of . . .' or that they had been 'donated by . . .'

It was at the end of the International Eucharistic Congress that you had your decisive encounter with Cardinal Gerlier.

Yes. Among all the cardinals who attended was old Cardinal Gerlier of Lyons. He insisted on speaking to me before returning to France. I was very busy by now organizing the assembly of Latin American bishops, so he had difficulty in tracking me down. But since he was a cardinal, and a

Frenchman, and a friend, we managed to arrange a meeting.

Cardinal Gerlier said to me: 'I was determined to see you because there's something I must say to you before I leave. I have had some experience in organization, and it's clear to me that the reason this congress has gone so well is because there was a talented organizer in charge. And that's the reason why I insisted on seeing you. May I speak to you as a brother, a brother in baptism, a brother in the priesthood, a brother in the episcopate, a brother in Christ? Brother Dom Helder, why don't you use this organizing talent that the Lord has given you in the service of the poor? You must know that although Rio de Janeiro is one of the most beautiful cities in the world it is also one of the most hideous, because all these *favelas* in such a beautiful setting are an insult to the Lord.'

And so the grace of the Lord came to me through the presence of Cardinal Gerlier. Not just through the words he spoke: behind his words was the presence of a whole life, a whole conviction. And I was moved by the grace of the Lord. I was thrown to the ground like Saul on the road to Damascus.

I kissed the cardinal's hands: 'This is a turning point in my life! I will dedicate myself to the poor! I'm not so sure that I have a particular talent for organization, but I will offer all the Lord has given me in the service of the poor.'

I went to see my archbishop and told him what Cardinal Gerlier had said. And I went on: 'To begin with, I should like to have all the wood that has been used for the Eucharistic Congress. None of it must be sold, at any price, or thrown away. We'll give it to the people here in Rio de Janeiro who have no shelter or homes. That's the first thing. And from now on, please let me dedicate myself to the *favelas* here in Rio. I will continue to give you all the assistance you require, but please let me dedicate myself first and foremost to the people who live in the slums.'

Had you not been particularly aware of the *favelas* until then? They were rather conspicuous, weren't they? ...

It's almost impossible to understand . . . I came from a fairly poor family myself, I came from the North-East, I had seen the effects of the droughts there. In Rio I came up against the world of the *favelas* at every turn. But the Lord had not been ready for me to be aware of them until now . . .

My cardinal gave his whole-hearted consent. I got together the people who had helped me so generously and efficiently in organizing the Eucharistic Congress, and we set to work. We founded the Saint Sebastian Crusade.

From the name alone you can see that we were still tied to the medieval attitudes of Christendom. We chose Saint Sebastian because he is the patron saint of Rio de Janeiro. But the word crusade . . .

At one point I had an audience with the Holy Father John XXIII. Obviously someone had spoken to him already about what we were trying to do in Rio de Janeiro, and he said to me: 'I understand you are working with the poor people in the . . . what are they called . . . *favelas*.' And I began to tell him, very proudly, about the Saint Sebastian Crusade. But he interrupted me: 'I can see you aren't familiar with the Near East! If you had been to the Near East you wouldn't have used the word "crusade" to describe the work of liberating the poor! Despite what historians often say, those accursed crusades opened up a chasm between us and the Moslems that is very difficult to bridge.'

What exactly did the Saint Sebastian Crusade do?

Well, as you will see: even with the best of intentions one can still make mistakes . . .

When we had finished distributing the wood from the Eucharistic Congress among the homeless, the essential problem still remained: all those *favelas* that sprawled over the mountain. So I went to see President Kubitschek, who was a good friend of mine, and said: 'Mister President, I want to tell you what has happened to me.' And I told him the whole story about Cardinal Gerlier. 'Now that my eyes have been opened I am haunted by all this misery.' And he said: 'How can I help you?' 'I have an idea, a suggestion that I'd like to put to you. When I saw the esplanade being built for the Eucharistic Congress it occurred to me that the same thing could be done in other places around the bay. But this time you could authorize me to sell the land reclaimed from the sea, and I could use the money to rehouse the people of the *favelas*.' 'It's a wonderful idea! I have no hesitation in saying yes. Please prepare the decree, and I will sign it at once.'

We decided to begin with one of the worst *favelas* in Rio: a slum that had sprung up like a mushroom right in the centre of the city, and in fact right in the centre of one of the richest and most elegant neighbourhoods. We set about building the new flats immediately next to the old slums. We felt that the way to transcend the class struggle was to bring the classes together. So we wanted the poor people to go on living right beside the rich.

The flats we built were by no means luxurious. They were very modest. But they were flats all the same. We set up a whole training programme to prepare the families from the *favela* for living in flats: they had lived in slums all their lives, and had never had running water or lavatories.

We also decided and made sure that as soon as each family was rehoused its old slum house would be demolished. Otherwise another family might come and take its place and the *favela* would simply be perpetuated. The *favela* was an insult to the Lord, and we really wanted to wipe it off the map.

Our plans sounded wonderful; but unfortunately they became embroiled in petty party politics. There was about to be an election. Every time we took a family out of the *favela* some politician would come along and put two or three or four families in its place. 'Wait there and Dom Helder will build you a new flat!' It was terrible. People could see that the Saint Sebastian Crusade didn't take long to build its flats; and they were all prepared to come and wait their turn in the slums. By the time our first project was completed we realized that instead of being wiped out the population of the *favela* had doubled . . .

So it was a failure.

From that point of view, yes, it was a failure. But our work did have one effect that we hadn't expected: the city of Rio de Janeiro finally opened its eyes to the *favelas*, and the authorities began to be concerned about them. We had forced them to take notice. Until then the problem didn't exist, because officially the *favelas* didn't exist. The *favelas* were never mentioned in urban development programmes: why bring in water and electricity? Why build sewers, since the *favelas* didn't exist?

And you had made them exist.

In a way, yes. Soon afterwards the governor, Carlos Lacerda, set about tackling the *favelas*, but he had a different method from ours. Instead of rehousing the families nearby, in the centre of town, he built the new flats a long way away, beyond the city limits, where the land was of little value – and where no one could object to the scheme. Because in fact the inhabitants of the smart neighbourhood where we had built the first ten Saint Sebastian's Crusade blocks of flats never forgave us for causing what they called 'residential pollution'. You can imagine why! The proximity of the *favelados*' flats lowered the value of their own properties...

I believe Carlos Lacerda drew attention to the fact that the root of the problem of the *favelas* lay not in Rio de Janeiro but in the countryside and that any effective campaign against the *favelas* must begin by bringing about basic reforms, particularly agricultural reform. Were you aware of his views?

Absolutely. It's a very accurate analysis. I understand it even better now that I am here in the North-East. Every day the agriculture industry expels more peasants from the interior. The big companies move in with their modern methods of cultivation which require far fewer hands and produce much higher yields. They buy vast tracts of land, and anyone who has been living there – probably without any official documents but often for several generations – is forced to leave. They're simply thrown out.

And they go to the towns. If they can, they go to Rio de

Janeiro or São Paulo. São Paulo has nearly eight million inhabitants. It's the largest city in the North-East: in other words there are more North-Easterners in São Paulo than in any other city in the North-East. The peasants think that they'll be able to find houses, schools, work, and hospitals in the city. And they finish up in the *favelas*.

So it's true that we need to attack the causes of this exodus and this misery, and that there can be no effective solution without agricultural reform. But that doesn't mean we should forget the people who are already here, the victims of unfair distribution of land and unwise industrialization of agriculture.

> The International Eucharistic Congress in Rio de Janeiro in 1955 resulted in your conversion to the poor, if I can put it like that. Did your work in the *favelas* in turn alter your attitude to the other events of a similar nature that you took part in subsequently? I'm thinking for instance of the International Eucharistic Congress at Bogota in 1968, which Paul VI attended in person.

I think that at Bogota we had the same faith in the presence of Christ in the Eucharist. But it was becoming clear to us that the Eucharistic Christ cannot accept an excess of glorification while the other Eucharist – Christ living among the poor – is oppressed.

One day a delegation came to see me here, in Recife. 'Dom Helder, a thief has broken into one of our churches and opened the tabernacle. Obviously he was only interested in the ciborium, and he threw away the hosts – threw them down into the mud! Do you hear, Dom Helder, the living Christ thrown into the mud! We have rescued the hosts and carried them in procession back to the church, but now we must have a great ceremony of atonement.' 'Very well, I agree. We will organize a eucharistic procession. We'll invite the whole diocese. And it really will be an act of atonement.'

On the day of the ceremony, when everyone was assembled,

I said: 'Lord, in the name of my brother the thief, I ask Thy pardon. He didn't know what he was doing. He didn't know Thou art truly present and living in the Eucharist. We are deeply shocked by what he did. But my friends, my brothers, how blind we all are! We are shocked because our brother, this poor thief, threw the Eucharistic Christ into the mud. But here in the North-East Christ lives in the mud all the time! We must open our eyes!' And I said that the best possible outcome of our communion with the Body of Christ in the Eucharist would be if Christ thus received would open our eyes and help us to recognize the Eucharist of the poor, the oppressed, the suffering. It was on this that we would be judged on the last day ...

At Bogota I was already aware of all of this. But the Eucharistic Congress was again very 'triumphal'. I don't blame my brother bishops of Colombia: their attitude was the same as mine had been a few years earlier.

After the International Eucharistic Congress in Bogota there was an assembly of the bishops of Latin America at Medellín. And there we undertook a radical revision of the concept of eucharistic congresses. It is still important that we human beings work to glorify the Lord. But what can we do? We can't make God any more God-like, any more powerful or glorious. We are miserable creatures! But we can help our fellow men, and help the poor. 'I was hungry, I was thirsty, I was in prison . . .' We can glorify charity; charity is God. But we must go beyond the surface of the words: it isn't enough to distribute food and medicine and money. Every century has its own particular way of seeing and enacting charity, according to the needs of the time. In our time charity is helping to make justice triumph.

We were blessed with the opportunity of holding a national eucharistic congress here in Brazil, at Manaus, in 1975. The bishops, priests, nuns, laity, all of God's people who took part helped to make the connection between the sacramental Eucharist and the Eucharist of the poor: appearance of poverty, real presence of Christ. At the most solemn moment of the Congress an unemployed worker, an abandoned wife with her children, and a prostitute spoke to us all. It was very moving.

And I think the International Eucharistic Congress that is being held in Philadelphia in 1976 will have a similar theme. Imagine being able to meet Mother Teresa of Calcutta and talk to her about the Eucharist of the poor! ...

14

FRIDAYS AT THE SECOND
VATICAN COUNCIL

Paul VI came to Bogota. Before that he had gone to
the Holy Land, Istanbul, and India. John XXIII
had been the first Pope to come out of the Vatican
for a very long time: he visited prisons in Rome and
made a pilgrimage to Lorette. It was a great event!
You must have been overjoyed to see the Pope out
in the world like this, among the people?

I have always dreamed of seeing the Pope, Peter's successor,
the supreme representative of Christ, travelling about like a
pastor, encouraging and fortifying his brethren. This was the
mission that the Lord entrusted Peter with: 'I prayed for
thee so that when thou hast overcome temptation thou canst
help thy brethren, and encourage them . . .'

But the Vatican State remains an anomaly. I understand
of course that the sovereignty of the little Vatican State
helps to ensure the independence of the Pope and the
government of the Church, but it causes dreadful anomalies.
The Pope tries enormously hard to travel like a simple
pastor, but he is always received like a head of state. And
it's just awful. I was at the airport when Paul VI arrived in
Bogota. All you could see was soldiers, soldiers, soldiers –
with machine-guns – all the way from the airport to his
residence. I have no wish to see the Pope come to Brazil
under these conditions, protected by machine-guns . . . I long
for the day when the Pope will really be just a bishop, the

president of the synod of bishops, the chief link in the collegiality of bishops, the head of God's people, and no longer a king . . . Then he will be able to travel without worrying about security and about risking his life.

I know that the Popes themselves – particularly the last ones, John XXIII and Paul VI, are the ones who suffer most from the errors of the past. It's obvious that they personally would prefer to be pastors rather than heads of state. I once saw something on television that made me very happy. Paul VI was being received at the United Nations with great ceremony by representatives from all the nations of the world. But he behaved so naturally! He came in, took off his cape by himself and gave it to someone, and sat down. He behaved just like an ordinary human being, just as if he were Peter himself, or Paul.

Oh, when will we manage to help the Church of Christ to liberate itself! If we're going to help to liberate the world we must work to liberate the Pope, and the bishops and all Christians . . .

I remember another significant episode. One day President Kubitschek sent for me and said: 'I want to ask you an enormous favour. I should like you to undertake a very important mission, but without any publicity. I want you to go to Rome as ambassador extraordinary. You will have two other ambassadors with you: the present ambassador to the Vatican and one of his predecessors who is here at the moment. You will go from here to New York first so as not to attract attention, and from New York you will fly direct to Rome. The Holy Father will be told that you are coming, and he will give you an audience. And this is the official message that I want you to deliver to the Pope: "The President of the Republic of Brazil has asked me to say to you that when a son is about to inaugurate his house, the house of his dreams, the house of his future, he invites his father even if he knows his father cannot come." Say to the Pope that Brazil is about to inaugurate its house: Brasilia. Brazil knows that the Holy Father will not be able to come. Nevertheless, Brazil feels it is its sacred duty to offer its Father an invitation".'

I listened attentively, and then replied: 'Mister President, your message seems to me so felicitous, delicate and Christian, that I am happy to accept the mission.'

So I set off for Rome with the Brazilian ambassador to the Vatican. The former ambassador who should have come with us was ill and unable to travel. John XXIII opened the door to us himself and said: 'Oh! They told me I was to receive a great archbishop, but it's a little one instead!' At first he smiled, but then he remembered that I had come on an official mission with the status and papers of ambassador extraordinary. 'Tell me then, how is the President of the Republic?' 'Holy Father, he is very well. And he has asked us, the ambassador and me, to convey to you a message which I found deeply moving – which is why I agreed to undertake this mission.' I repeated President Kubitschek's message word for word. As he listened, John XXIII was visibly moved. When I had finished he repeated three times: 'I must go to Brazil. I must go to Brazil. I must . . . But unfortunately, it's impossible . . .'

We have to liberate the Pope . . .

> This audience took place before the Council?

Yes.

> Was it on this occasion that you described how you envisaged the Pope travelling not only to Brazil, but to Jerusalem, the meeting point of Orient and Occident, North and South? Later you applied this vision to the closing ceremony of the Second Vatican Council, which you saw taking place in Jerusalem. You even wrote the scenario for a spectacular celebration that symbolized the reconciliation of all mankind, all races and all religions . . .

The closing ceremony that I envisaged never took place: the Lord's imagination is not the same as ours. But I didn't have to wait until the end of the Council for my dream to come true. As you know, Pope John died during the Council. Do you remember the anguish that was felt all over the world while he was ill? Catholics and Protestants, Jews, Buddhists, Moslems – everyone, people of every faith, without exception, experienced an intense sense of unity throughout his long agony. The Lord had chosen the death of Holy Pope John to bring mankind together.

As the Council drew to a close many of the delegates began to hope for some kind of prophetic development; in fact quite a number of us were thinking of standing up in Saint Peter's Basilica and proclaiming John XXIII a saint. We were sure that the new Pope Paul VI would stand with us. But while we were debating the best way to proceed our Protestant brethren who were there as observers pointed out our mistake: 'Be careful! If you canonize John XXIII you will create problems. Because John XXIII didn't just belong to Catholics: he belonged to all of us. It was God's plan that he belong to all men: don't annex him for yourselves!'

> Dom Helder, unless I am mistaken you didn't speak once in the auditorium during the entire Council: you didn't intervene at all.

That's right.

> Why was that? You aren't normally afraid to speak in public . . .

That's another story altogether . . .

Before the Council, when my cardinal got back to Rio de Janeiro from a preparatory meeting in Rome, he said to me: 'Everything is all right, my son. The Lord has chosen the best person for every office. The secretary-general of the Ecumenical Council is just the man we need. He will conduct the Council like a maestro conducting an orchestra.' He was very pleased. However, I was rather anxious. Because I pictured the Ecumenical Council as a manifestation of true episcopal collegiality, with Peter and under the guidance of the Holy Spirit, not as the performance of an orchestra with its violinists, harpists, clarinettists and so on under the direction of a maestro.

All of the Brazilian bishops who had been elected or delegated to the Council arrived together in Rome. The government paid all our travelling expenses, there and back. That was consistent with the logic of relations between

Church and State: by attending the Council we were rendering a service to our country.

We arrived four days before the Council opened, and immediately I got a message from my old friend and brother and co-vice president of CELAM, Dom Manuel Larrain – Manuelito, as I called him. He wanted to speak to me. I have never quite managed to understand how that man knew as much as he did. It was as though he had antennae.

Monsignor Larrain had heard that the secretary-general was going to address the Council on the opening day. He would welcome all the Conciliar Fathers, and then say that the Pope had asked that eleven commissions might be set up to initiate the work of the Council, and that each commission should consist of sixteen bishops elected by the delegates and four bishops appointed by the Pope. He would add that it would be appropriate that each commission include representatives from as many countries as possible. And then he would explain that unfortunately the delegates were not yet familiar with the bishops from countries other than their own; so he would ask the Council to put the matter in the hands of the secretary-general and vote at once for the lists he had already prepared.

'If we agree to his suggestion,' said Monsignor Larrain, 'we shall soon be no better than that orchestra your cardinal was talking about.' So we tried to think of a way of preventing a procedure that might seriously interfere with the exercise of episcopal collegiality. We both agreed that only cardinals could offer resistance to the secretary-general of an Ecumenical Council. What we had to do was persuade about ten cardinals to stand up one after another and reply to the secretary-general: 'No, let us wait for a few days so that we can get to know one another; and then each Episcopal Conference can propose those of its members who seem best qualified for each commission.' We compiled a list of ten cardinals. We knew that first of all we must win the support of the French bishops, because without them we would have very little influence. We went to San Luigi dei Francesi and spoke to Monsignor Veuillot, Archbishop of Paris and president of the French Episcopal Conference, and Monsignor Etchegaray, the secretary of the conference, a most distinguished man. Both of them agreed with our plan and offered us their whole-hearted support. We shared out the list of ten cardinals between the four of us, and we each began to make visits.

So the opening day arrived. You probably know how Saint Peter's Basilica was arranged. The bishops were divided into groups of one hundred, and between each group was a gangway and a small staircase. When the secretary-general of the Council began to speak there was already a seminarist standing at the head of each staircase waiting to distribute the lists of names the secretary-general had prepared, and the papers for voting. Everything was ready to go according to the plan. But when the secretary-general sat down Cardinal Liénart, the old Cardinal of Lille, stood up and turned to Cardinal Tisserand, who was presiding: 'I should like to speak!' 'But that's impossible!' Cardinal Tisserand replied, 'I can't allow you to!' 'I shall speak nevertheless. I have listened to the secretary-general's suggestion, but we simply cannot accept –' and so on. There was thunderous applause! And then Cardinal Tisserand said: 'The Council is only just beginning and none of us has any experience of such a Council. We have to formulate our own rules. I should like to propose that we ban both clapping and whistling.' There was another tumultuous outburst of applause: we were like schoolchildren on holiday!

After Cardinal Liénart a second cardinal stood up to speak, then a third, and a fourth. After the sixth one had spoken the secretary-general returned to the tribune: 'We are here only to carry out the decisions of the assembly. You are the Conciliar Fathers. You have the last word. You and the Holy Father, guided by the Holy Spirit, have complete power.' The elections were postponed for four days.

But I still don't understand why you never spoke . . .

I'm coming to that. But you have to understand the background. Immediately after the opening session Monsignor Larrain and I agreed that we should call a meeting of all the delegates from the Latin American Episcopal Council, CELAM. Latin America was the only continent where the bishops were already organized and accustomed to working together. We weren't planning to propose Latin American bishops for each of the eleven commissions, but to consider in which of the commissions we could offer most assistance. The meeting had to take place on the same day.

We went to see Monsignor Miranda, Archbishop of Mexico and president of CELAM. But he disagreed with us: 'It's impossible! I have had a letter from the Pontifical Commission for Latin America. Taking into account the experience of earlier councils, and in order to prevent national blocs forming, the Commission asks that no CELAM meetings be held while the Council is in session.' I replied: 'My dear Monsignor Miranda, I have known ever since I was in the seminary that while a Council is in session the Roman Curia does not govern the Church. Only the Conciliar Fathers with Peter, under the guidance of the Holy Spirit.' 'But I dare not . . .'

So we went to see a Latin American cardinal who we knew would agree to summon a meeting of the CELAM delegates at about four o'clock on that same day at the Salesian house where they were staying. It was Cardinal Silva Enriquez of Santiago in Chile. He did agree, and we distributed notices of the meeting. It didn't take long for us to agree on a list of the bishops we felt were best-qualified for certain of the commissions. We were the first group to be able to put forward a list of suitable candidates like this, without any pretensions. During the next four days there was considerable dialogue between the episcopal conferences, and as a result several outstanding bishops who had not previously been known outside their own countries, such as Monsignor Zoa from the Republic of the Cameroons, were elected to the commissions.

I felt that this initial dialogue between the episcopal conferences should be continued. The Brazilian bishops were staying at the Domus Mariae, where there were several large rooms well-equipped for meetings and wired for sound. I suggested that we make our residence available for informal meetings, say, every Friday, where each conference could be represented by one of its key members. The purpose of the meetings would of course be to assist the work of the Council.

The Friday meetings worked very well, with the providential assistance of Monsignor Veuillot and Monsignor Etchegaray. Officially CELAM was the host; but in effect it was the French conference that did all the work, and made arrangements for photocopying, telephones, and general administration.

The meetings helped to keep people informed and gave them an opportunity to work out and express their opinions in preparation for important debates. Our aim was always to assist the work of the Council, never to sabotage it.

> But your ideas of what was best for the Council and for the Church were not shared by everyone? ...

Well, we wanted to help the Church and the Council to move in what we saw as the direction of the great encyclicals, in the direction taken by John XXIII, and it was working very well. But at a certain point we discovered that the secretary-general of the Council had become suspicious of our Friday meetings, which he saw as secret meetings of conspirators. So then we realized that we needed a cardinal to be our patron.

The Pope had appointed four moderators to preside over the Council. One of them was Cardinal Suenens, Archbishop of Mechelen in Belgium. Our estimation of him increased from day to day. It was he who lighted the way of the Council by defining the two great axes of the Church 'ad intra' and the Church 'ad extra'. I was asked to speak to him, and ask him to be our patron. I went to see him in the Basilica, and said: 'I have a letter for you.' 'Well, read it to me.' 'No, Your Eminence, it makes a great deal of difference whether I read it to you now or leave it with you and come to see you this evening to talk about it.'

It was a very simple letter explaining what our Friday meetings were, the suspicions they had, and the need we felt for the patronage of a cardinal to make it clear that we were working not against the Church, but to assist the progress of the Council. Cardinal Suenens acknowledged that we were making a very serious request. 'But tell me frankly,' he said to me, 'I know that you are a personal friend of Cardinal

Montini. Why don't you ask Cardinal Montini to be your patron?' 'It's very simple. It seems to me that although the Lord has bestowed on Pope John the responsibility and glory of opening this Council, he will not be blessed with the privilege of closing it. So . . .' And strangely enough, Cardinal Suenens suddenly said: 'Excellent!' But he added: 'Do you trust me?' 'Your Eminence,' I replied, 'I used not to trust you. You didn't understand Catholic Action and you opposed it. I disagreed with you and I opposed your ideas. But you are no longer the Cardinal Suenens I used to know. You are another Suenens. And I have come to ask for the patronage of this Suenens, moderator of the Council, whom I trust completely.'

This frankness between us gave birth to a friendship that grows stronger with every year. While I was in Brussels recently we were talking about the Charismatic Movement, of which he is the leader. He showed me some reports, some booklets he had written to sustain the movement in the freedom of the Spirit, while warning against radicalization and divergence. He showed me a first, second and third booklet. But I said: 'You need a fourth booklet as well, to explain the indispensable link between the movement of the Spirit that leads us to prayer and the movement of the Spirit that leads us to serve others. Even the Charismatic Movement must beware of alienation.' 'That just shows how well in tune we are with one another,' he replied. 'We're on the same wavelength! I have already begun to write the fourth booklet. Look, I use exactly the same words: avoid alienation, make a link between prayer and service.' We really saw eye to eye.

During the Council my dear Father Michel, as I called Cardinal Suenens, gave us just the support we needed. He defended us whenever our Friday meetings were liable to be misinterpreted. Since he was in a key position he was able to warn us when he saw problems approaching in the Council, and suggest what we might do to solve them.

So you see all of this was my answer to your question. I had all this work to do which I felt was very important, and consistent with the occult apostolate. I felt this was enough and that I didn't need to intervene in the Basilica.

Invisible presences played an important part in the Council. Most important of all perhaps was the invisible presence of Pope John. Even after his death he was still living among us. I was also aware of the invisible presence of Teilhard de Chardin: some of the great theses of the Council are positively Teilhardian . . .

> There was another group at the Council called 'The Church of the Poor'. Was that also a pressure group?

In many cases it was the same bishops who were involved in both groups. I am very fond of that name, which comes from our French brethren: 'The Church of Poverty and Service'. The Holy Spirit has called us and brought us together. He has opened our eyes to the duty of Christians, but especially of pastors, to imitate Christ, who although He belonged to all men identified Himself with the poor, the oppressed and all those who suffered. We have begun to look for a way of making the whole Church, but first of all each one of us individually 'poor and serviceable'.

As I have already told you, I didn't realize at that time that true poverty is not the kind we choose but the kind that God sends. I thought for instance that the clothes I wore could be a sign of poverty. But then the photographers used to follow me everywhere. I realized that external poverty is worthless unless it is a manifestation of internal poverty. There is a real danger of pride in humility: 'Look at me! I am a poor bishop, a bishop of the poor! I am not like those bourgeois bishops.' That is terrible. You see it wasn't until later that I knew that the poverty God had chosen for me was not to take away wealth – which in any case I didn't have – but to snatch away my fame, my reputation, my prestige.

> You mentioned the invisible presence of Teilhard de Chardin at the Council. Other people at the time talked about the influence of Freud. There was a campaign to persuade the Church to recognize

> psychoanalysis. Did that interest you, or did it seem
> a rather marginal, secondary matter?

Although I respect psychology, psychoanalysis and psy-
chiatrists, I must say straight away that it is not one of my
principle concerns. Everyone has his own obsession . . .

> And that isn't yours?

No.

> At the time the Council was hailed as a decisive
> event, a 'springtime for the Church', full of promise
> for the future. Now the future is here and, in
> Europe at any rate, all we hear about is the crisis in
> the Church, and the crisis of faith. Were people
> mistaken about the fruitfulness of the Council?

You know, if you look at the history of the Church, you find
that every great Council has been followed by a crisis. There
are always some people who hang on to the past and make it
their duty to defend the true Church. They exaggerate. And
there are always others who exaggerate in the opposite
direction. Balance is something that men find very difficult.
It isn't surprising: the Creator brought together several
different worlds in one creature. We are brothers to stones,
trees, animals, angels, and God Himself. And these different
worlds cause conflict and struggle within each of us.

Attitudes and structures were so profoundly shaken by the
Council that it would have been inconceivable for every-
thing to go smoothly, quietly and harmoniously afterwards.
It would have been disturbing if there hadn't been collisions
and clashes and conflicts: it would have meant that the
Council had said nothing and done nothing.

As far as I am concerned the backwash of the period after
the Council is not the real problem. The real problem, I
repeat, is our lack of courage when it comes to putting the
conclusions of the Council into practice – or, for us Latin
Americans, the conclusions of Medellín: in other words,
putting into practice the Gospel as we bishops, with the

Pope and under the guidance of the Holy Spirit, have interpreted it for the people and the world of today.

I know that many people talk about a crisis of authority in
the Church, and even a crisis of faith. My personal experience has taught me that a crisis of authority is most
likely to come about when the authorities haven't the
courage to accept the consequences of the resolutions they
have studied, discussed, voted for and ratified. If there is a
crisis of authority it may also be because we who are in
authority forget that exercising authority means serving, and
not being served. Authoritarian authority is impossible
nowadays: authority can stem only from dialogue and
mutual, fraternal, consideration.

A crisis of faith happens only when we are afraid and say:
'Watch out! Man is going too far! He is trespassing in God's
domain. Look: soon he'll want to be able to create life, and
conquer death! He has already gone so far as to modify the
human brain, make the human heart beat artificially and
violate space! God cannot permit it: these powers belong only
to Him!'

But I can't imagine that God is jealous. Jealousy seems to
me a sign of deficiency: you are jealous when you want
something you haven't got. Well, I should feel very sorry for
God if He had to be jealous of man! We must keep going.
We've hardly begun to respond to the Lord's invitation to
participate in nature, and in His creative power. Why
should we be afraid? ...

> You refer frequently to the assembly of Latin
> American bishops which took place in Medellín, in
> Colombia, in 1968. This assembly at Medellín
> marked the emergence of a new theology known as
> 'the theology of liberation'. What is the theology of
> liberation?

When you look at our continent, where more than two-thirds
of the people live in sub-human conditions as a result of injustices, and when you see that the same situation is repeated all over the world, how can you help wanting to
work towards human liberation? Just as the Father, the

Creator, wants us to be co-creators, so the Son, the Redeemer, wants us to be co-redeemers. So it is up to us to continue the work of liberation begun by the Son: the liberation from sin and the consequences of sin, the liberation from egoism and the consequences of egoism. That is what the theology of liberation means to us, and I see no reason why anyone should be afraid of a true, authentic theology of liberation.

15

'LIBERATION' IN AID OF 'DEVELOPMENT'

In the fifties you were 'the bishop of the *favelas*'; in the sixties and seventies you have become 'spokesman for the Third World'. What made you adopt this new role? Was it Bandoeng and the irruption of the Third World on to the international scene? The overthrow of Batista by Fidel Castro? The war in Indo-China? The encyclicals *Pacem in Terris* or *Populorum Progressio*?

Certainly all of these events made a deep impression on me, as they did on the whole world.

Personally, as I think I have already told you, I became very involved in the idea of 'development'. The word conveyed a hope for solidarity and for real collaboration between rich and poor countries. The increasing gap between the minority of rich countries and the majority of poor countries might be bridged. But it very soon became evident that the developed countries' resolution to set aside one per cent of their gross national product for aid to underdeveloped countries was not going to solve the problem. And that the problem would also not be solved by raising this figure to two, three, or even four per cent. Paul VI was courageous enough to say that what the developed countries gave with one hand they took away with the other.

When I speak of aid from developed countries I always distinguish between private and official aid. I am always grateful for any disinterested help from our richer brethren. While we are fighting to secure justice, this help enables us to rescue the victims of injustice and save them from a miserable death. But I am very fearful of official aid, which eases the donor's conscience, and gives the impression that everything that can be done is being done, while the heart of the problem is forgotten. And the heart of the problem, of course, is the unjust politics of international commerce. At the end of the first 'decade for development', President Nixon himself was forced to admit that the rich countries were emerging from the decade richer and the poor countries poorer.

I remember one occasion when a government minister in the German Federal Republic had the idea of holding a forum on development. He invited representatives from all the political parties, Churches and universities in the Republic. There were also representatives from all the major West German associations and business concerns, including the multinationals, and representatives of youth organizations. I was officially invited to speak on behalf of the Third World, and to declare the conference open.

I said that the Third World was being oppressed from within by internal colonialism and from without by the unjust politics of international commerce. I said that if the rich countries had the courage to trace the roots of their wealth they would see that they were buried deep in the misery of the Third World.

At the end of the conference the representative of the association of writers and artists asked the Minister what he thought of what the guest of honour, Dom Helder Camara, had said. The Minister replied very intelligently, quoting the statement made by Richard Nixon at the end of the decade of development. Then one of the youth representatives stood up and said: 'All of this is true, sir, and we are grateful for your frankness. But now we have to go further. We have here among us representatives of three major companies: the Deutschebank, Mercedes-Benz, and Volkswagen. It would be very useful for us and very instructive, if they could tell us how much their companies have invested in the Third World during, say, the last ten years; and how much profit they have made on those investments.' The

representative of the Deutschebank was extremely indignant:
'You see, Minister, this is what happens when you invite
children to talk with adults!' This was greeted by a storm of
catcalls. I would never have thought that Germans could
make such a noise: it sounded more like the Maracana
stadium in Rio when a football team does something wrong.

I took advantage of the momentary confusion, and since I
was guest of honour took it upon myself to speak. 'Minister,
I always say that when I am in a foreign country I never feel
like a foreigner: it's true that I am a Brazilian and a Latin
American, but wherever I go I am still a human being; we
are all children of the same Father; and therefore we are all
brothers and sisters. May I say that I find this demonstration
of freedom wonderful? Germany has not always enjoyed
freedom like this. If I may make a suggestion, I hope you
will preserve this atmosphere of freedom throughout the
forum. And I should like to suggest to the representative
from the Deutschebank that the important thing is not to
know whether someone is a child, an adolescent, an adult or
an old man. The important thing is to appreciate the weight
of an argument.'

The youth representative stood up again and said:
'Minister, we must excuse our colleague from the Deutschebank. When you are forced to spend all your time dealing
with money you are bound to lose your sense of humour. But
we don't in fact need to importune our colleagues from the
major companies, because we have here their official
reports.' He proceeded to read out the figures showing how
much money had been invested in the Third World, and how
much profit had been taken from the Third World: and the
whole audience was deeply shocked.

The United Nations Conferences on Trade and Development – UNCTAD – were another profound disappointment.
The plan had raised high hopes at first, because it looked as
though the United Nations might set up a special agency to
investigate the problem thoroughly.

One UNCTAD, then another UNCTAD . . . We were
there, trying to mobilize the young people from the richer
countries so that they would urge their representatives to
adopt a clear and courageous position. Either the famous

Prebisch Report was wrong, and must be shown to be wrong; or it was right, in which case the industrialized countries couldn't go on simply proposing aid of one per cent, two per cent . . . They must propose and accept measures to ensure justice in international commerce.

But in assemblies like UNCTAD it isn't only the delegates from developed countries who present a problem; sometimes the delegates from poor countries are, or behave like, representatives of the privileged classes in those poor countries, which isn't at all the same thing.

I remember for example the attitude adopted by the Brazilian delegation at the third UNCTAD, at Santiago in Chile. These delegates gave the impression that Brazil no longer considered itself an under-developed country, but rather a candidate for the Club of Ten – or at least the Club of Twenty. Fortunately Mr Robert McNamara, president of the World Bank and former United States Minister of Defense, took us all by surprise. He spoke about the increasingly unfair division of revenue in the under-developed countries; and he even had the courage to use the example of Brazil to illustrate the growing gap between the small group of rich people and the mass of poor people. I don't suppose the Brazilian government was very pleased. But it was true, and the speaker was a man above suspicion.

This is why 'development' was such a disappointment to us. We had had such high hopes – Father Lebret, whom I chose as adviser at the Council, François Perroux, Paul VI. Now we prefer to speak of 'liberation'.

> Do you regard Fidel Castro's liberation of Cuba as a
> model for the whole of Latin America?

For a long time the young people of Latin America were fascinated by what had happened in Cuba. It looked as if the Cuban solution might be the solution for the whole of Latin America, and perhaps even for the whole of the Third World. Groups of young people all over the world, I think, began to consider the possibility of guerilla warfare, because guerilla warfare was what had liberated the Cubans from Batista's dreadful dictatorship.

We know how guerillas work: they lure regular armies into areas where modern weapons and conventional tactics are useless.

When Fidel Castro and Che Guevara went underground the United States was totally unprepared for this kind of warfare. And so were their allies. But the Pentagon immediately set about helping the Latin American armies to form and train special units equipped to fight guerillas. It wasn't long before the 'Cubanization' of Latin America was out of the question.

I must say that I personally never saw Cuba as a solution. Because changing orbit isn't really liberation: becoming a satellite of Russia instead of a satellite of the United States.

> As far as one can tell the change of orbit wasn't what Fidel Castro or the Cuban people wanted: it came about because of American politics.

True. And any hopes that Latin America might be Cubanized were finally crushed on the day when the United States, threatening nuclear attack, reminded Russia of certain agreements made between the Great Powers in Yalta, at the end of the Second World War: Latin America was under the influence of the United States, not Russia. Then Russia instructed Cuba for the time being not to press for the Cubanization of Latin America. So the underground and the guerillas couldn't expect any more help from Russia. And now young Cubans, manipulated by Russia, go off to fight in the wars in Africa, rather like young Portuguese in the time of Salazar had to go and defend the 'overseas territories', or like young Americans had to go and kill or get killed in Vietnam . . .

> One man who certainly believed that Latin America should be Cubanized was the Colombian priest, Camilo Torrès, who became famous when he joined a Communist underground group and was later killed in an ambush. Did you know him?

Not personally. I think Camilo Torrès was one of many young priests and laymen who lost faith, not in Christ, but in the institutional Church, when they saw all the fine resolutions of the Vatican Council trapped by human weakness and ecclesiastical prudence. Like others, Camilo Torrès believed that the only way he could really help to liberate his people was through guerilla warfare, and he chose to join a Communist underground group. I also think that the Colombian Communists took advantage of Torrès' reputation and deliberately sent him on a mission where he was likely to be killed. For them the end justified the means. The end was to make known and to popularize the existence of the guerilla movement. The means was to have a celebrated martyr.

Camilo Torrès died, and neither the young people nor the workers of Colombia came forward to help the guerillas. Our Colombian brethren were very frustrated.

But you see it was like Che Guevara's failure in Bolivia. Che Guevara had a natural genius for guerilla warfare, and he had seen its effects in Cuba. But his mistake was to forget that a mass of people is not the same as a united people. A mass only becomes a united people after a long and difficult campaign during which the people are gradually and quietly made more aware. The majority of Bolivians, like nearly all Latin Americans, were living in sub-human conditions; but since they had no reason for living they also had no reason for dying. The Bolivian peasants welcomed Che Guevara and his men because they were armed. But afterwards, when the government soldiers came, they welcomed them as well and told them everything they knew about the guerillas and their hiding places.

All of this only made me more and more certain that liberation could never be achieved through armed struggle. Young people would often come to see me, convinced that violence could be effective, and I had to take a pencil and paper and spell it out to them: 'Friends! Let us suppose that a group of you decide to rob a bank to get enough money to buy arms. To begin with, when you get to the bank, you run the risk of either getting killed yourselves, or of killing a bank employee, some poor man who works there to earn a living but has nothing to do with the system. But suppose you are successful, and you manage to get away alive and without killing anyone. You might have, say, five hundred thousand new *cruzeiros*. So? How many rifles, pistols, machine-guns, and rounds of ammunition can you buy with this sum? And how effective are these weapons going to be against the enormous supplies of armaments that the Pentagon supplies to our governments, and which form a major part of the supposed aid to under-developed countries? And another thing: where are you going to buy your weapons? From whom? And how are you going to import them? How are you going to train people to use them, people who have no experience of fighting? My friends, there is no point in taking up arms against the forces who manufacture arms and wars.'

And they would always reply: 'Yes, but give us one example of a country that has managed to liberate itself without violence.' And I would say: 'Give me one example of a country that has managed to liberate itself with violence.'

> They could have said Vietnam, Algeria, or, more recently, Angola ...

Yes, but as soon as they were politically liberated these countries fell prey to new masters. You could say the same of a country like India, which achieved its independence through non-violence. Political independence without economic independence is not really liberation. Economic power wields powerful and effective weapons. Remember what happened in Chile. Allende made it clear from the beginning that the socialism he envisaged for his country was not aligned with Moscow, Peking, or even Cuba. It was a form of socialism adapted to the needs and aspirations of the Chilean people. But ITT and other multinationals were there. At one point it even looked as if the divisions and quarrels among the left which paralysed Allende might have been secretly provoked and kept alive by economic interests. In Latin America we have two hundred and fifty years' experience of political independence without economic independence. The forces that need poor countries, and need poor countries to stay poor, are very skilful at exploiting the weaknesses of people who are ill-prepared for liberty. That is always the aftermath of victory.

In fact, when we talk about liberation, whether through violence or non-violence, we are groping in the dark . . .

> One day in February 1948 you wrote somewhere that your whole day and part of your night had been taken up with Gandhi. I presume it was the news of Gandhi's assassination that moved you so much. Was that the beginning of your commitment to non-violence?

No, I don't think there was a particular day when I began to believe in non-violence. It has always been my way of interpreting the Gospel – my temperament, if you like. But I don't really like the expression 'non-violence'. I much prefer Roger Schutz's phrase: 'the violence of pacifists', or any other definition that emphasizes the contrast with 'passivism'. How can we expect young people to renounce armed violence unless we offer them something strong and effective in exchange – something that can achieve concrete results?

I have always tried to find a way of changing unjust structures through the application of moral pressure. For a long time I believed that this moral pressure could come from institutions such as the Churches, the universities, trade unions, the press . . . All one had to do was make them aware of the problem and mobilize their strength.

One day I was talking to a European head of state whom I respect a great deal, and who I believe is a true Christian. We were discussing what he could do to help the Third World, and he asked me to make a concrete suggestion. So I suggested that he call together the vice-chancellors and department heads of the principal universities in his country, both private and public, and ask them to undertake a serious critical study of the Prebisch Report. Raul Prebisch was the secretary of the United Nations Conference on Trade and Development, and the report he compiled demonstrated the disastrous results of the first half of the so-called decade for development, 1960–70. It was an impressive document that showed quite clearly how, under cover of international solidarity, the rich were becoming richer and the poor poorer.

If the professors, with all their competence and scientific authority, concluded that the Prebisch Report was to be taken seriously, I suggested that they in turn invite their colleagues from other universities throughout Eastern and Western Europe and the United States to join them in the study and decide what conclusions might reasonably be drawn from the results of the alleged worldwide politics of development.

In my opinion this mobilization of the universities would be the beginning of a major shift of public opinion. The media would be there immediately echoing the academics. Because the media would be prepared as well: they would be given all the relevant documents, and the special correspondents from every major newspaper and radio or television station would be thoroughly briefed.

I also suggested that the cardinal-primate of the country, a most distinguished man who was universally respected, invite representatives of all the Protestant denominations, Judaism, and atheistic humanists, to prepare joint conclusions on behalf of the major religions. I am always concerned not to separate atheistic humanists from the major religions. I disagree with those who say that atheistic humanism is doubly atheistic: because it denies God and because it puts man in God's place. It seems to me on the contrary that the true atheistic humanist fulfils at least half of the Law: he loves his neighbour. And if you love mankind sincerely, then without knowing it and even without wishing it you also love God.

And then I saw the movement extending to include representatives of employers' federations, and representatives of workers' federations, at both national and international levels.

But your dream didn't come true?

No. I was forced to accept that institutions as a whole are too cumbersome to be manipulated like that. It isn't easy to mobilize even a single university: it's impossible to mobilize several. And it's the same with Churches, and trade unions...

So then I discovered minorities. It's true that all the

various institutions taken as a whole are difficult to move; but it's also absolutely true, experimentally demonstrable, that in every institution, every human group everywhere, no matter what the country, race or religion, there are minorities who, beneath a vast diversity of denominations, leaders and objectives, share a common hunger and thirst for justice: minorities for whom justice is the path of peace. I call them 'Abrahamic minorities' in honour of Abraham, the father of all those who over the centuries have continued to hope against hope. But I should like to find a more universal name for them: Jews and Moslems and Christians know Abraham, but Abraham means nothing in the East. I now believe that the moral pressure to liberate mankind will come not from institutions as a whole, but from the minorities that I still call Abrahamic.

> At one point you tried working with Ralph Abernathy, the successor and heir to Martin Luther King. In 1970 you signed a covenant with him.

I have always seen, and I still see, the Negro movement in the United States as an outstanding example of active non-violence. Martin Luther King Junior achieved great victories within the United States. His successor, Ralph Abernathy, actually came here to Recife on one occasion, to invite me to come to the United States and receive the Martin Luther King Prize. I was very touched by that. But I said to the brothers of Martin Luther King, and the brothers of Ralph Abernathy, that they must extend their struggle. Because the battle against racial discrimination in the United States was only one aspect of the struggle to liberate the Third World. They must go on, but they must go further afield.

> The 'peaceful violence' movements that have been most effective, in the Indies, or in the United States, have always been inspired and guided by particular leaders, powerful personalities with whom the movements to some extent identified themselves: Gandhi, Martin Luther King, Cesar Chavez, and so on. Dom

> Helder, why have you always refused to play this
> role of leader, either in Brazil or in the Third
> World?

I have in fact been asked several times. At one point our
friends in Holland made an attempt to bring together the
leaders of active non-violent movements all over the world.
They wanted me to lend my name to the meeting and be, if
you like, the leader of leaders. But I refused.

It isn't a leader that we lack. The action of one man, or
even one organization, will not make the minorities strong.
The Holy Spirit has inspired all of these different groups
throughout the world, and only the Holy Spirit can make
them effective. The vast audiences that I find wherever I am
invited to speak are united by a common desire: not to see a
particular man, or hear a pop singer, or join an organization,
or adopt a slogan. What they share is the same hunger and
thirst for justice as the path to peace.

What we lack – but it will come, certainly! When God
undertakes a task He wants men to collaborate with Him;
but He helps us, He doesn't abandon us – what we lack is a
way of creating links between the minorities, and of uniting
them – without unifying them – in common aims. It will
come! And I am sure that the solution, the method, will
come from young people. We have already seen some
practical examples.

In England, in Germany and in Switzerland certain
groups of young people resolved to bring pressure to bear on
the multinational companies who had their headquarters in
those countries. By getting together and making sacrifices
they were able to buy a few shares in the companies. This
entitled them to attend the annual general meetings. They
got hold of complete lists of shareholders, and sent letters to
every one saying: 'Dear Sir or Madam, like you we hold
shares in this company. As shareholders, like you we hope to
make a profit from our investment. But we are sure that like
us you do not wish to make a profit out of human suffering.
So we would ask you to make every effort to attend this year's
annual general meeting, at such and such a time and place,
and give careful consideration to what we are going to say

there, to the statistics and arguments that we are going to present.' But of course the management of the companies quickly found a way of excluding the young protesters.

In Canada we began another experiment. I was invited there by the five largest Christian denominations in Canada, who every year organize what they call 'Ten Days for Development'. I told them about the young people's frustrated efforts in Europe, and added: 'Perhaps the major Christian denominations can succeed where these young people failed. The Christian Churches very often invest in multinationals. It's quite understandable: they have to maintain churches and clergy, often subsidize social work, and finance missionary expansion; and in order to make sure that the money people give them does not lose its value they have to invest it and invest it well. So they are enmeshed in the system. If you have money invested in multinational companies, I would ask you to leave it there for the time being. But you can take advantage of your position: ask for detailed information about how the company's profits are earned. It's far more difficult to get rid of the Christian Churches than a group of young people. They have far more money, for one thing; and they have considerable moral influence. If the Churches together obtain detailed information; if together they discover that the profits of major Capitalist enterprises derive from the oppression of human beings, if together they draw conclusions from their findings – it *must* set off a worldwide movement for justice.'

But perhaps it is still too soon to ask religious leaders to do this, even Christian leaders. Again, we must be patient, and work at making them aware of the problem. This is what the Christians and other volunteers began to do in the United States in preparation for the bicentennial year, when they asked somewhat awkward questions about the justice and liberty which Americans vow to guarantee all men.

I distrust choices and decisions that are made in high places, without the participation of the people. Take the study of the 'new international economic order', for example, which the United Nations has finally managed to set up. It's highly significant as it proves that something must be wrong with the current international economic order, otherwise we wouldn't be looking for a new one. But I'm quite sure it won't be long before the 'experts' take over, the economic powers interfere, and the new international economic order will be conceived and defined from the top, without any assistance from the people. It will be a mockery of a new economic order: a new mask, in effect, for old imperialism. And the oppression will continue as before.

That is why we need the minorities to be present, vigilant and active. And always hopeful. I cannot believe that a world created by a God who is love, liberated by the Son of God who is love, and sustained by the Holy Spirit who is love, will ever give itself up to selfishness and hatred. It's impossible!

> In October 1968 you set up an active non-violent movement in Recife called 'Action for Justice and Peace'. What was the outcome of this initiative?

Very often we begin a task, make plans, draw up a programme for the future – and then it transpires that the Lord has other plans.

I saw 'Action for Justice and Peace' primarily as a way of organizing moral pressure for liberation within Brazil, and specifically in the North-East. But it was the Lord's wish, particularly after the Fifth Institutional Act was passed in December 1968, that any movement of this kind was rendered practically impossible. But at the same time He let me receive a very large number of invitations from abroad. I get an average of eighty invitations a year. Of course, I can't possibly accept them all. But through travelling abroad I have discovered that there is injustice, and there are active minorities, all over the world, and not just in North-Eastern Brazil. The name isn't important: but 'Action for Justice and Peace' has switched from a local and national plane to an international plane.

> I should like to come back to your travels later. But I wonder first if you could describe the occasions and the circumstances in which you have encountered socialism. It has been clear for several years that

> you would prefer some kind of socialist solution to
> the problems of the Third World. That isn't an
> attitude you acquired in the seminary!

I must say first of all that I have never been to a socialist
country. I am not speaking of the countries where socialism
is really a new, advanced, form of Capitalism. The only
invitation I have ever had from Eastern Europe came from
Yugoslavia. I was asked to give lectures at the universities
in Zagreb and Ljubljana. The Yugoslavian ambassador
came to see me, but even before I opened the envelope
containing the invitation I said to him: 'Forgive me, Your
Excellency, but I must make it clear to you at once that I
will never go to a country where I shouldn't have the right
to speak freely. The only country in which I am prepared to
live without freedom is my own.' 'When you read the
invitation you will see that you are guaranteed total freedom,
even to criticize the regime if you wish.' 'Well even if I had
no problems with your government I should certainly have
problems with my own. If they consider me a Communist
and a subversive when I visit only Capitalist – even super-
Capitalist – countries, just imagine what they would say if
I were made welcome in a socialist country!' So I didn't go
to Yugoslavia.

But I know how Capitalism works. And it's become
absolutely clear to me, and to many others in the Third
World, that there is no hope of our people being liberated
through Capitalism. Of course there are different kinds of
Capitalism: but in every Capitalist system the concern with
profit takes precedence over concern for people. Even when
they say: 'All you have to do is wait! First we must develop
the economy, then we'll tackle social reform!' It's still profit
that comes first. And it's clear that the most advanced
element of Capitalism, the multinational company, makes the
privileged classes richer and the poor poorer.

So we look instead towards socialism. We are not naive.
We can see the distortions of socialism that make Russia,
for example, with its thriving bureaucracy and Stalinism, one
of the most compelling arguments against socialism. But we
believe that tomorrow or the next day – and I hope it's

tomorrow if it can't be today – young people will succeed in creating a system of humane socialism, quite different from the Russian anti-model. I can't speak about China because really we don't know enough about it, here, in Latin America. I simply have the impression that it still isn't ideal. We must find a new way.

As a Christian, a Catholic and a churchman, I am devoted to my Mother, the Church. And it's because I love her that I am so demanding. I don't like it when she disillusions people, and disappoints them, particularly young people. And I wonder how much longer she is going to keep arriving too late.

I remember how we ridiculed the word 'republic' at first, and how long it took before we could use it seriously! And the word 'democracy': that was forbidden, too! So why on earth should we ban the word 'socialism' from the modern Christian vocabulary? Why pretend that socialism is necessarily tied to dialectical materialism? Why claim that socialism is always anti-religious and anti-Christian? I remember the great effort Pope John had to make in order to be able to talk about 'socialization': that was his way of talking about socialism without using the word! It's ridiculous for the Church to remain trapped in this fear.

I remember the first time I met Roger Garaudy. We were both taking part in a conference organized by an American movement which was trying to provoke new ideas and initiatives based on John XXIII's encyclical *Pacem in Terris*. After we had worked together for three or four days I realized that basically Roger Garaudy and I looked at things in the same way. We were brothers.

So I said to him: 'Roger, shall we make a pact? I want you to promise me two things.

'As you know there are some Marxists who make Marx their idol. They think that being a Marxist means simply repeating, word for word, what Marx said, and doing what he did. They don't realize that, being a realist, Marx would look at things differently today.

'For example, they go on saying that religion is necessarily linked to alienation: but it isn't true. I am the first to admit that in the past, and unfortunately still today, certain religious groups have presented religion in a very passive way, precisely as an opium for the people, and in doing so they have caused alienation. But I assure you that in every religion, not only in Christianity, there are individuals, groups and minorities who are working to make religion a liberating force rather than an alienated or alienating one: a force that can liberate mankind from sin and the consequences of sin, from selfishness and the consequences of selfishness. If you can accept that, please try to stop Marxists automatically linking religion with alienation. That is the first point.

'And secondly, do you think socialism is necessarily tied to dialectical materialism, or is it possible, as I believe it is, to be a true socialist without adhering to dialectical materialism?

'For my part, I promise to do all I can, and to get other more influential people to do what they can, to make the Church accept socialism.'

And have you adhered to the pact?

Yes. Both of us have done our best. But we haven't quite succeeded yet . . .

Paul VI wrote a letter to Cardinal Roy in which he spoke explicitly about socialism – without condemning it . . .

Yes. That was quite a step forward. Paul VI is intelligent, and sincere. He is very aware of social problems. But he is subjected to enormous pressure. He gets all these letters and reports which always emphasize the dangers, the perils, the negative aspect of things . . .

Quite apart from your pact, did you get on well with Roger Garaudy?

Yes, I respect him a great deal. I can remember another experience we shared.

German television was preparing a remarkable series of programmes. First of all they had made films about Asia,

Africa, Europe, North America and South America. And then they brought together in West Berlin a panel of two Buddhists, two Shintoists, two Hindus, two Moslems, two Jews, two Christians and two Marxists, to comment on the films. We all stayed in the same hotel. And for a whole week we spent every afternoon watching and discussing a film which was particularly relevant to one or other of the religions represented. For example, after we saw the film on Asia, the Buddhists, the Shintoists and the Hindus were asked: 'What have you done, what are you doing, what are you trying to do, to help these people?' The films were very powerful, showing human suffering and oppression in each continent. After the African film it was mainly the Moslems who were questioned, and so on.

I knew that our turn would come with Latin America, and I knew what I had to say. Everyone on the panel had been very sincere. We didn't try to hide our faults or our sins of omission. We tried to explain why we had failed to realize all our aims, ideals and expectations; but the reality was there in front of us, and we were there to admit it. It was a terrible disgrace to religion, to every religion.

Marxism was represented by a young Yugoslavian journalist, and by Roger Garaudy. It was obvious that the young Yugoslav was delighted by everything he was seeing and hearing. And when it was his turn to speak we were not surprised to hear him say: 'Forgive me, my friends. But after thousands of years the extent of your achievements in the service of humanity is pathetic. I am proud to say that in half a century Marxism has transformed Russia from a semi-feudal country into a rival to the United States!'

It was then that we had another opportunity to witness Roger Garaudy's profound integrity. We knew that he had remained faithful to Marxism, faithful even to the Communist Party. He had resisted the temptation to form another party, which might have caused division among the workers. But it was this fidelity that gave him the strength now to reply to his Yugoslavian colleague: 'My friend! Everything that you have said is true. But you have forgotten one thing: the terrible price that Russia has had to pay!' And he went on to describe the horrors of bureaucracy, and Stalinism, and so on.

I remember another occasion as well, when I saw the famous encounter between Cardinal Daniélou and Roger Garaudy on French television. With respect for the memory of Daniélou, I must say that it was Garaudy's remarks that seemed particularly impressive. I love him for his sincerity. In one of his recent books he says at one point that he feels to all intents and purposes that he is a Christian, but he has never dared to call himself a Christian. He feels that being called a Christian must be terribly demanding, and he hasn't the courage for it. But in another book he acknowledges that he is a Christian.

> That's *Parole d'homme* [*Word of Man*]. But I imagine another thing that brings you and Roger Garaudy together is your common love of poetry, and artistic expression, and even dance.

Yes, you're right. I enjoy seeing Garaudy gradually discover the immense power of dance, and painting, and poetry, and film. How could a Marxist like this, a free man who loves freedom, help being expelled by Stalinist bureaucracy?*

I remember that when he showed me his first film he said he was already working on a second one, but that it still wouldn't be the film of his dreams. The film of his dreams would be a film that portrayed a wonderful prophet who works desperately hard for his cause, and risks his life repeatedly. But at a certain point the prophet succumbs to the temptation to become king, and that is the end. To me that is an expression – in lights and movements and images, with all the power of the cinema – of what happens so often with socialism. Socialism is the prophecy of modern times. But when it comes to power . . . Even the Soviet Union is beginning to give way to a consumer society. Without having the courage to admit it, the Russians are adopting a banking

---

*Roger Garaudy was expelled by the General Committee of the French Communist Party in 1972.

system, and multinational companies are establishing bases there just like everywhere else. There is so much deception ...

But all the same, despite human failings, I remain hopeful. I'm not saying we shall ever create Paradise on earth; but gradually, generation after generation, we will create a world that is freer, more just, more humane.

16

ALL DICTATORSHIPS
ARE TERRIBLE

In 1964 you were appointed Archbishop of Olinda
and Recife. It meant returning to your point of
departure, the North-East. But at the same time,
just a few days beforehand, the Brazilian 'revolution'
took place – the military *coup d'état*. I know that you
and other informed bishops were expecting some kind
of political turning-point in Brazil. But did you expect this revolution to establish itself as it has, to
become institutionalized, and to last this long?

Yes, it became perfectly obvious in the end that the extreme
right, particularly within the army, was bound to react
against the moves made by certain politicians, and particularly by the President of the Republic, João Goulart.

João Goulart was a curious figure. He got his political
philosophy from Getúlio Vargas. He was very rich and
owned a great deal of land in the South. But he had inherited the 'friendly dictator's' sympathy for the people.
He was probably being manipulated from one direction or
another: but it became fairly clear that he was planning a
revolution. He wanted to remain friendly with the generals,
but he relied on the sergeants. He wanted to keep up a
dialogue with the employers, but he relied on the workers.
He thought he could count on the CGT*, as if the CGT were
a reality; whereas in fact all the country had experienced in

* *Comando Geral dos Trabalkadores.*

terms of trade unionism was *peleguismo*: when the authorities disapproved of a representative elected by the workers because he had ideas – it was a serious offence to have ideas – or because he had the courage to speak out – and it was a serious offence to have the courage to speak out – he would simply be replaced by a shop steward appointed by the minister . . .

Eventually President Goulart made his famous 'speech to the sergeants'. It was broadcast over the whole radio and television network. As soon as we heard it, Cardinal Motta, the president of the National Conference of Bishops, in São Paulo, and I, who was secretary-general of the conference, in Rio de Janeiro, felt that we must try to see the President of the Republic immediately, to put him on his guard and warn him against making any rash moves. Because the proposals he had made did not seem to us to constitute a serious programme of structural reform, nor a firm basis for establishing a truly humane socialist system, but rather a kind of sentimental leftism which had no particular aims but would almost inevitably bring about a military reaction, or in other words, a dictatorship.

We tried to make the president understand this. But unfortunately he seemed to have no sense of reality. He was convinced that the generals were behind him, as well as the sergeants on whom he relied. And he talked about the solidarity of the CGT. 'But Mister President,' we said, 'there is no CGT in Brazil!' He didn't believe us.

It had been agreed that this meeting would be strictly confidential. But at the end of the meal a photographer came into the room and took a photograph of the cardinal, the president, and myself. The cardinal and I protested, but João Goulart assured us that the photograph was intended only for his personal archives. But three or four days later this photo appeared in the newspapers. And three or four days after that the army seized power.

> The photo must have given the impression that you were Goulart's allies?

More than allies: intimates. There we were giving the president advice and plotting with him . . .

> Could you not contradict the accusations, and tell the truth?

But you see this man had just fallen from power, he was utterly defeated: we didn't want to add to his suffering. This wasn't the moment to say: 'No! The reason we went to see the president was precisely to try to open his eyes to the danger! He may be sincere but he is terribly naive! We were there to try to prevent a catastrophe!' No, we couldn't do that. The cardinal and I decided to accept the consequences.

But my transfer from Rio de Janeiro was not one of the consequences. It is simply untrue to say that the army forced me to leave Rio.

> So it was pure coincidence?

My transfer had already been arranged. My cardinal in Rio de Janeiro sensed that the gap between his attitude and mine on open questions, particularly social questions, was growing wider all the time. He had read the chapter in the Acts of the Apostles where Saint Paul tells Barnabas that it would be better for them to part: 'Look, here are two saints, two great saints, and despite their holiness they decided to separate!' I was very glad. I attach great importance to loyalty between human beings, and particularly between priests and bishops. From that moment on I made every effort to ensure that I left Rio de Janeiro as soon as possible.

My departure for Recife coincided with the 1964 revolution. But I didn't see it as a coincidence. I believe it was Providence that opened this new chapter in my life. I came back to the North-East, but now I saw it differently. Coming back to Recife, I saw it as one of the key points of the Third World. Recife is one of the capitals of the Third World and a whole new horizon, a whole new vocation, opened up before me. While remaining a faithful servant to the Church of Christ that is here, in Olinda and Recife, I realized that it was impossible to solve local problems unless the countries we depended on were converted: and that the Lord had called me to missionary work on an international scale.

Was there any relationship or continuity between the lieutenants who had led the 1920 and 1930 revolutions and the 1964 generals? Are the generals of today the lieutenants of yesterday, promoted and older, but with the same ideas?

In the Brazilian army the official retiring age is sixty-five. In the beginning, after the 1964 revolution, some of the 1930 leaders were still in evidence – Eduardo Gomès, for instance, and Juarez Távora. But the Fifth Institutional Act of 1968 marked the victory of a new generation and a new mentality. It also marked the passage from a romantic revolution to a technocratic or at least a supposedly scientific revolution.

The technocratic revolution claims to base its ideology of *Segurança nacional*, National Security, on the so-called geopolitics of Brazil. Everything is conceived in terms of National Security. To begin with, the two major perils, corruption and subversion, must be eliminated. Afterwards a development programme will be put into action, designed to conform with the requirements of National Security.

The basic idea is that a Third World War is inevitable. The enemy, of course, will be Communism. The United States will ultimately win the war, and therefore Brazil must remain allied to the United States. But unfortunately – Brazil regrets this fact, but has to be technologically prepared for it – the United States will emerge from the Third World War just as debilitated as Great Britain was after the Second World War. So according to Brazilian geopolitics the next world power, the next empire, will be Brazil. That is the official theory behind the government of Brazil.

On the basis of this theory Brazil must first prepare to exercise the 'leadership' which geopolitics shows to be its natural role in Latin America. All the plans for trans-Amazonian roads, hydro-electric engineering, energy development ... are seen as a function of this natural 'leadership'.

The model chosen for economic development was a neo-Capitalist one. The cake had to be cooked before it could be shared out. The people must first go through a period of austerity. Wages were strictly controlled. The people had to tighten their belts; but the privileged classes got more privileges. Exports had to be developed. For the ruling classes things went very well. They even spoke of a Brazilian economic miracle. But among the people we saw increasing proletarization and more malnutrition. I say this without any hatred. I have nothing against the military, absolutely nothing. But it's because I love Brazil, this place that the Lord made my home, that I find all this so terrible.

Later it became clear that the so-called Brazilian economic miracle was just an illusion. But then all the experts said it was the world oil crisis and inflation that had caused the problems, and the Brazilian development policy was still sound. All we had to do was start again: whatever happened, Brazil was still destined to be the next empire! ...

If only I could make people understand that it's precisely because I love Brazil so deeply that I don't want it to cherish this foolish dream! ... As I said before, I dream of a world without empires. Why must there always be empires, one after another? Even our dear Portugal had its empire. And Spain, and Holland, and Britain, and France, and the United States ... Why, O Lord, can we not achieve a world without empires, without oppressors and without oppressed? ...

> Did the 1964 'revolution' in Brazil have any connection with what was happening in other Latin American countries where democracies were overthrown by authoritarian regimes – Uruguay, Argentina, Chile, Ecuador, Peru? Not to mention Paraguay. Is Latin America doomed for some reason never to have a viable democracy?

The word democracy, in relation to Latin America, has a very special meaning. Governments in Latin America are said to be democratic because there is an executive power, a legislative power and a judiciary power; because in theory the three powers respect one another; because in theory the legislative controls at least the major activities of the executive; and because, again in theory, the judiciary power has the last word. But in fact the people who hold office in these three powers belong to the same privileged group. That makes for a very unusual sort of democracy. Of course more or less the same situation exists in the so-called true democracies. Pure democracy, ideal democracy, doesn't exist anywhere, does it?

Nevertheless in these rather special democracies there was a certain freedom of movement, freedom of speech, freedom to have opinions, to write and to hold meetings. You see a great difference when a democracy, even a very imperfect one, gives way to a dictatorship.

Dictatorships, whether of the left or of the right, are always terrible. There is always a climate of suspicion which poisons even private life. Everything is controlled and spied on. You don't know if the man who was your friend yesterday will denounce you tomorrow. I have heard that under Hitler and under Stalin parents were forced to betray their children, and children their parents. But this practice didn't end with Hitler and Stalin. You hear stories about life under Communist regimes, behind the Iron Curtain, and it sounds horrific. But the fact is the same methods are used here as well. There's very little difference. Here, just as in every other dictatorship in every country and every age, so-called subversives are arbitrarily arrested and tortured. Tortured so that they will give information that is supposedly vital to National – and even Continental – Security! When will people realize that it's impossible to rely on information extracted by means of torture?

Of course we Catholics, heirs to the Inquisition, stand as a sorry example. In fact if you compare the instruments of torture used today with those used by the Inquisition, there isn't very much difference. Only in the days of the Inquisition there was no electricity. Burning was done directly with fire. Electric shocks are far more subtle . . .

It's impossible to understand how man can have remained so primitive – on both sides: in the East and in the West, in dictatorships of the left and of the right, in the name of the Security of the Regime, or in the name of National Security – in an age when he is exploring space, conquering disease and mastering cybernetics! What can we do to wake people up and make them realize what's happening?

As long as force has to be used to defend human rights we

are trapped in a vicious circle. This is true on an international level as well: as long as we have to resort to United Nations troops to keep the peace there will be no end to war. That is why I believe that the numerous small countries in the United Nations must unite. They are already beginning to realize that together they can form an obstacle in the path of the major powers. At some point they have to challenge, refuse, the right of veto. It's ridiculous, the right of veto! It's totally undemocratic! It simply negates the principle of the United Nations. The day I am waiting for, the day that will mark the beginning of the great advance of active non-violence, is the day when the small countries forget all their petty selfishness and petty quarrels, and say unanimously to the major powers in the United Nations:

'From this day, from this hour, there will be no more of this incredible, undemocratic right of veto exercised by the Great Powers! There must be no more great ones and small ones here: either we are all great, or we are all small. But we are all brothers!' And I don't believe the United States will dare to fight to retain its right of veto. And I don't believe it will be easy for the Soviet Union to threaten to withdraw if the right of veto is abolished. It will be simpler for both the United States and the Soviet Union to accept the decision and then, perhaps, to withdraw their financial support from the United Nations. So then the United Nations would have to find a way of financing itself and meeting without relying on the wealth of the Great Powers, without being manipulated by the wealth of the Great Powers. Because that is really what is happening at the moment. The President of the United Nations and the Secretary General of the United Nations are the dollar and the rouble! . . .

> The campaign against subversion which followed the military *coup d'état* in 1964 was obviously aimed particularly against militant Christians, priests, nuns and even bishops. Would you call it persecution, or is that too strong and too anachronistic a word?

In order to really explain the situation, I must first have the courage to confess the sins of omission that we churchmen committed. Once again I should say that I have no wish to blame any individuals, and above all I have no wish to judge the past by present standards.

The churchmen in this country and in this continent used to be so preoccupied with upholding authority and the social order that we were incapable of seeing the terrible injustices that were and still are perpetuated by this so-called social order. The Christianity we preached was too passive: patience, obedience, acceptance of suffering in union with Christ. Great virtues, of course: but in the context they merely reinforced oppression. And during all this time, the governments and the great landlords were pleased and proud that the Church guaranteed them this support.

But when we opened our eyes to the brutal reality, after the social encyclicals, the Second Vatican Council and Medellín, it became impossible for us to continue in the same way. It came as a great surprise to the proprietors of the established order when their traditional ally, the Church, turned against them. More and more Catholic laymen, priests, nuns and even bishops began to denounce the injustices – at least, the most serious injustices – in Brazil. According to the theory of National Security, this makes them agitators and subversives. And we have to accept the consequences.

> Very costly consequences: how many priests have been deported? How many laymen imprisoned and tortured? How many bishops put under surveillance?

It isn't only Christians. Communists are also hunted down, arrested and tortured. The Communists are very impressed when they meet Christians in prison. They thought religion was a thing of the past. They never imagined that Christians, priests, nuns, and laymen, might be prepared to suffer torture for a love of justice, the poor and the oppressed. And the Christians in turn are astonished when they see the courage and strength with which these Communists face the most terrible tortures – men who have only dialectical materialism to make them hope for a better world.

But there isn't only official terrorism. There are radical revolutionary groups who also resort to terrorism. I have never been able to understand, much less sympathize with, methods like the taking of hostages. As far as I am concerned, the end can never justify the means. And it's important to see the repercussions of this kind of terrorism as well. For instance every time there is a revolutionary terrorist incident in a neighbouring country, in Argentina, say, or in Uruguay, the Brazilian media are instructed to emphasize every horrible detail of it; and the government takes the opportunity of intensifying repression so as to protect the nation against these new forms of banditry.

> Dom Helder, you yourself have been directly affected by the campaign against subversion. Firstly you have been condemned to silence, reduced to the state of a zombie. And secondly, which must have been far more painful, you have been attacked through your collaborators: they have been used as hostages to obtain your submission.

Yes. The most painful time for me was just after the lecture I gave in Paris in 1970.

Propaganda in Brazil says that I spend all my time travelling abroad: but it isn't true. As I mentioned to you before, I receive an enormous number of invitations, but I accept only about four or five each year, and I am away for just over a month of every year.

It also isn't true that I travel abroad and give lectures in order to attack Brazil, my own country. I would never do that! I travel and lecture in order to fight against injustice, and to show that justice is the path of peace. And as I said before, I never feel like a foreigner, wherever I go. When I am in the United States, I speak out against what I see as unjust in United States politics with total freedom. And it's the same when I go to Germany, Britain, Belgium, France – anywhere in Europe. There are no longer any 'internal' problems, problems that are peculiar to one country and are of no concern to 'foreigners'. Everything is linked now, and the problems of the individual are everyone's problems.

When I went to Paris in 1970, at the invitation of the Catholic Committee of French Intellectuals, my friends there immediately began to question me about what was happening in Brazil, particularly about the tortures which had been reported in the French press and all over the world. This was before the lecture I was due to give to an enormous audience in the Palais des Sports. I knew that if I didn't have the courage to speak honestly about what was happening in our country I would lose the moral authority and strength I needed to denounce the injustices that the French should be fighting against, both at home and abroad. So I told them the truth. I spoke out, not against my country, but against the tortures.

From that moment a vicious campaign of defamation was launched against me in Brazil. I was absolutely forbidden to deny or defend myself against the accusations in any newspaper or magazine, or on any television or radio station. Later they decided that it was a mistake to attack me publicly, and the media were simply forbidden to mention my name. I was and am condemned to civil death: I don't exist. But I have come to accept it.

I don't know how I would have reacted to torture. There's no way of knowing. I never blame people who weaken under torture. It's impossible to imagine how one would be affected by being crushed, and beaten . . . Nevertheless I believe I would infinitely have preferred to be tortured myself than to have my collaborators tortured. Anyone who has children can imagine what it is like for a father to know he is free and safe while his sons and daughters are hunted down, arrested, put in solitary confinement and tortured instead of him.

> Or even assassinated, like the priest Enrique Pereira Neto . . .

Yes, assassinated. It's absolutely horrible. The number of times I have had to go to hospitals or prisons, or even to a morgue, to collect or identify collaborators who had disappeared – priests and laymen . . .

In all fairness I should say that these attacks on me by way of my friends, which went on for several years, have now ceased. My collaborators are no longer threatened. But the people are still oppressed. I don't mean simply tortured. I mean they are still suffering from poverty and hunger, and the effects of unfair distribution of revenue. And I don't mean only in Brazil: the victims of injustice are all over the world.

17

IN THE NAME OF THOSE
'SEM VEZ E SEM VOZ'

Have you ever thought that the Nobel Peace Prize could have helped you in your work? You were formally proposed as a candidate for the Prize three or four years in a row; but each time the Norwegian Parliamentary Commission chose another laureate. It was a great disappointment to your supporters every time, but particularly on the last occasion, when the Commission chose Mr Kissinger and Mr Le Duc Tho instead. Were you equally disappointed?

When I was little I was taught that it is very important to know how to win and how to lose. When I played football and my team lost I used to hate all the recriminations: 'But there were twelve in the other team! It was the referee's fault!' and so on. I hated that. It's important to be a good loser.

I didn't get the Nobel Prize. Why challenge the jury? The decision must be respected and accepted.

But you know there was quite a reaction on my behalf, particularly in Scandinavia. And they created the People's Peace Prize for me. There was a very moving ceremony in Oslo – rather solemn and grand – and then the prize was presented to me at Frankfurt, in West Germany. That was a more informal occasion. The money was collected all over Europe – in Norway, in Sweden, in Finland, in Denmark, Germany, Holland, Belgium and France. The People's

Peace Prize was to be worth as much as the Nobel Prize, and have the same significance. It was very impressive. But I couldn't agree to the Scandinavians' first idea, which was to create an 'Anti-Nobel Peace Prize'. I prefer 'The People's...'

But I never accept prizes as if they were intended for me, Dom Helder, as if I personally had earned them. I consider myself simply a representative of the vast numbers of people fighting courageously for justice in obscurity, without ever seeing their names in the newspapers or their faces on television. On all those ceremonial occasions I am really just the little representative of a great legion ...

Was the People's Peace Prize actually worth as much as the Nobel Prize in the end?

No: two and a half times as much!

And what did you do with the money?

I discussed it with the groups who had collected the money, and with my collaborators here, and we decided to invest the People's Peace Prize in agriculture in the North-East. We bought several pieces of land, and we are experimenting with the advancement of agricultural workers and diversification of produce. On one small sugar-cane farm we are demonstrating that it is possible for workers united in a kind of co-operative to compete effectively with the big estates. The co-operative does everything: there are no intermediaries. The workers aren't concerned about living like lords. The whole project is intended to teach the people to run their own business.

In the other *engenhos* we are experimenting with diversification of produce. If you put all your efforts into one product there is a great danger that its price may suddenly drop. Especially if it is a raw material. The prices of raw materials are determined far away from here in the great commercial centres. The price of sugar may be at one level today and suddenly drop tomorrow. The United States may decide for instance that it is in its interests to resume relations with Cuba. So we have persuaded the farmers to experiment with diversified production.

Do these *engenhos* belong to you? Or to the diocese?

No, no. They were bought by our Operation Hope. But then they were handed over to the workers.

How much land is involved?

The sugar-cane project is on a small farm at Cabo. For the diversification project we bought two *engenhos* with the money I received for the Peace Prize, and joined them together.

One thing that has given me enormous pleasure in these last few years is the interest the neighbouring farmers have shown in these projects. They come to visit us, and they're quite astonished. It's better to be good neighbours than enemies . . .

It's difficult, and slow, but we are progressing. They are only small experiments. In a way we're repeating what we did twenty years ago in the *favelas* of Rio de Janeiro. We are attracting attention and proving that it really is possible to help the oppressed escape from oppression without becoming oppressors themselves.

As far as you know are there any other experiments going on in the North-East like the ones you have set up?

There are experiments everywhere! . . . I can imagine that to people who hear me on the radio or see me on television or read about me in books I must sound like a voice from another world when I talk about the Spirit of God. But it's real! The ideas and plans for helping the cause of human advancement aren't isolated, in some remote corner of the world. The work of making people aware and the defence of human rights are not monopolized by one man or one movement. It's a current running through Brazil, Latin America, the whole world, everywhere where there are minorities and grass roots communities. And that is the basis of our hope. Not only for the Church, but for humanity. Liberation won't come from above. It will come from below, from the people. And all the grass roots communities are conducting experiments in liberation and in human advancement, under all sorts of different names.

> You receive prizes. Every year you also receive several honorary doctorates. I find that curious as academic ceremonies, scrolls and medieval insignia don't seem to go with your personality. But you still accept the honours.

I believe you already know the story of my first 'doctorate'. One day I went to speak to some ordinary people in a parish on the outskirts of Rio de Janeiro, Engenho Novo. Afterwards the old parish priest stood up to thank me: 'I don't know how to thank you, my dear brother, Doctor Helder Camara . . .' 'But my friend, I am not a doctor.' The old priest apologized to the audience: 'He says he isn't a doctor!' But then someone in the middle of the room stood up and shouted: 'He is a doctor!' And the whole audience rose and repeated with him: 'He is a doctor! He is a doctor!' So then the priest concluded: 'You are a doctor now, my friend, by proclamation of the good people of Engenho Novo!' That 'doctorate' will always be the most dear and precious to me. But since then there have been other, more official ones.

> At first they were mainly doctorates in theology, then doctorates in social sciences, and now, more often than not, they are doctorates in law, in recognition of your work for human rights. What prompts you to accept these honours?

Since I am still considered a subversive and a Communist in Brazil, it is encouraging and helpful to be acknowledged in this way by universities who are not only not suspect, but frequently quite prestigious. It may help people to understand that the ideas I am trying to spread are not entirely crazy.

> St Louis, Louvain, Harvard, the Sorbonne – they certainly are impressive references. And it seems as if every time another institution honours you it

inspires you with an appropriate idea. I believe the Brazilian army still calls its military college 'the little Sorbonne'. And I imagine that was the reason why when you came to Paris to receive the honorary doctorate in law at the Sorbonne you put forward your proposal for the Peace Colleges . . .

Yes, but the origins of the idea go further back than that.

Paul VI once said that it was wrong to go on repeating the maxim of the Ancient Romans: 'If you want peace, prepare for war.' He contradicted this so-called wisdom: 'No! If you want peace, prepare for peace!' And that is what I said at the Sorbonne. I also suggested two projects that the Peace Colleges might tackle immediately.

At one point during the Second Vatican Council we were preparing a declaration that totally condemned war. But then a delegation of North American workers came to Rome and said: 'Please don't condemn all wars outright, because that might cause an economic collapse, and large-scale unemployment.' And it's true that generally speaking the democracies are not capable of surviving without their war industries. So I suggested that a Peace College might set up an interdisciplinary study of the possibilities of converting war industries, and of the conditions necessary for peace industries to be economically viable.

The second example I gave concerned the fixing of prices in international trade. When the Arabs decided to fix the price of their oil themselves people were amused at first. But when they realized the Arabs were serious Kissinger went so far as to threaten them with war! The problem of price fixing is very serious and complex. It requires very careful, delicate, and objective study. Here is another challenge for a Peace College.

The phenomenon of war, the process of war, is incredible. I am a member – a non-scientific member – of SIPRI, the Stockholm International Peace Research Institute. I receive all sorts of information through SIPRI: we know for instance that Russia and the United States already have in stock more than fifteen times what it would take to destroy all life on earth. And yet both Russia and the United States continue to augment their destructive powers – qualitatively if not quantitatively. Even the democratic countries who are not or who are no longer empires, like Belgium, or France, consider it not only their right but also their duty to prepare for war. They have already been defeated once or twice; they see the arms race continuing around them; and they too are obliged to arm.

There is a terrible, infernal logic about the arms industry. The cost of manufacturing armaments is so high that you can only afford to make them for yourself if you can also sell some to other countries. You have to sell. Naturally there is no question of selling to the United States or the Soviet Union. So you have to approach the poor countries, the Third World countries and the countries who haven't the means to feed all their people. And you encourage these countries to enter a mini arms race, a ridiculous but terrible race. SIPRI has impressive dossiers on the sales of arms to the Third World. As you know modern weapons become obsolete very quickly. A bomber that was perfectly adequate two years ago will now, after two years, be out of date. And it's the same with machine-guns and missiles. So the arms salesman can come back and say: 'You know, in the interest of National Security . . .!' And insinuate, and suggest, as salesmen do: 'You know, your neighbour is preparing for war; he's just bought some of the latest weapons!' All to make the poor countries buy. But if the salesman comes three or four times, and predicts the imminent, certain outbreak of war three or four times – and the war still doesn't happen, there's a danger that the governments of the poor countries may have doubts: 'But why are you always warning us about war? It's an obsession!' And they may stop buying new weapons. So then a war has to be manufactured. That's the infernal logic: you begin by manufacturing arms to defend yourself, then you sell arms so that you can carry on manufacturing them, and then you are forced to manufacture wars so that you can carry on selling the arms that you are obliged to carry on manufacturing . . .

You aren't always presented with a prize or an honorary doctorate on your trips abroad. Most of the time you simply give a lecture. You have given a great number of these lectures. I know that you prepare each one very carefully. Obviously you are often expected to deal with the same themes. But some of your lectures represent a very precise, direct challenge, which would normally provoke a response or at least a reaction. I am thinking of what you said at Louvain about the new responsibilities of theologians; and at Chicago about how you believe Saint Thomas would have understood Marx in the same way that he understood and in a way baptized Aristotle. I am thinking of the idea you put forward at the Sorbonne, which you have just described, of setting up a Peace College; of your lectures at Bonn and Brussels on the responsibilities of the countries that belong to NATO and the European Economic Community, particularly with regard to the sale of arms; and of your lectures at Berne and Zurich on the good and bad use of neutrality and money ... Do you ever hear any echoes of these challenges, that make you think they have at least been heard?

On one occasion, in Switzerland, I expressed certain doubts about the country's neutrality: and I got quite a powerful reaction. I hadn't realized, but apparently there is a clause in the Swiss constitution which forbids foreigners to challenge the country's neutrality. All I wanted to do was to stimulate ideas through discussion. We did have a fruitful discussion. And it is to the Swiss government's credit that I was not forbidden to return to the country afterwards. It didn't stop me saying what I thought: 'Even Switzerland is manufacturing arms! Even Switzerland is selling arms! It's incredible!' Just like Sweden, a traditionally neutral country, which manufactures and sells arms! ...

But in general the response to the challenges I put forward wherever I go comes not from institutions, but from minorities. Minorities recognize what I say: because even if I give the impression of having my own ideas, I am really an echo myself of the groups of people everywhere who are working and looking for solutions.

> You were saying that you receive an average of eighty invitations a year and that you accept only five or six. How do you decide which ones to accept?

When I receive an invitation I consider first of all whether the lecture I am asked to give or the meeting I am asked to attend will give me the opportunity of meeting the active minorities in the country or region. This has happened in different ways for example in Belgium, the United States, Switzerland, and so on.

At the same time I need an assurance that I shall have absolute freedom of speech. I know that people sometimes suspect I am not free. But unless I am guaranteed absolute freedom I don't accept the invitation. I remember one occasion when I was invited to speak in Florence on the occasion of the march organized by *Mani tese* – 'Outstretched Hands'. When I arrived at the airport in Rome I was met by the representatives of five more radical groups, who said to me: 'You must not compromise yourself by speaking to these young people: their march, the whole demonstration, is financed by multinationals! You mustn't do it!' But I assured them: 'My friends, if I had had the least indication that my freedom of speech would be restricted in coming here, I would not have accepted the invitation. But I am completely free. And I am going to speak in Florence about multinationals!' And I did speak about multinationals. On two other occasions I received invitations from Capitalist organizations: once from Brussels, the heart of the EEC, from an association called 'Business Ventures of the Future'; and once from Davos in Switzerland, from the Fourth Forum of European Business Executives. In both cases I was offered complete freedom of speech, so I accepted the invitations.

And obviously I try to make sure that the meeting I am being invited to is likely to encourage and stimulate new ideas. I have no wish to be a tourist, or some kind of show-business personality!

Let me describe one of my recent trips, so you can see the kinds of things I do. Towards the end of 1975 I went away for ten days. First of all I went to the United States. I had been invited to the university of Cincinnati to receive an honorary doctorate in law and also the Saint Francis of Assisi Prize. That gave me the opportunity of speaking, at the university, about the challenge Saint Francis offers to people of the twentieth century. The next day I went to St Paul, Minnesota, to address a meeting of five thousand teachers who were making preparations for the bicentenary of American Independence: 'Liberty and justice for all!' The next day I went to Davenport, where I received a prize intended to encourage people who are campaigning against racism. I was also given a calumet by a group of North American Indians; and a group of hippies gave me a very beautiful medal and the title 'citizen of the world'. Then I crossed the Atlantic and went to Amsterdam, where I was made a doctor *honoris causa* of the Free Protestant University. From Amsterdam I flew to England, where I gave a lecture to some university academics in Leeds, and then went to London to receive a peace prize which was presented to me in the Queen's Chapel by Lord Mountbatten, the former Viceroy of India. Lord Mountbatten and I are the two non-scientific members of SIPRI. And finally I went to Belgium to take part in a public debate with my brother Suenens, to give a lecture at the university of Courtrai, to attend a meeting of young people in the Cathedral Sainte-Michel in Brussels, and in the evening to take part in a discussion with the most active minorities in Belgium.

So that was a trip lasting ten days. Experienced travellers will appreciate the effort involved in the change of climate, the time difference and speaking French and English. Especially when you take into account the fact that it's only my hands that speak those languages well; the rest comes as best it can from my heart, from a hunger and thirst for dialogue.

I can see and understand that, to young people especially, it may look ridiculous of me to accept all of these prizes and honorary titles. But it's never for myself that I accept them. I never for one moment forget that I am simply the representative of the people *sem vez e sem voz*, 'with no hope and no voice'. It is these people, the poor, the humble, the oppressed, who are heard and honoured through me.

And the audiences are wonderful: they get bigger all the time, and there are always many young people. Why?... Why do they have the patience to listen to my almost unintelligible English or French? The only possible explanation is harmony: all of us long for the same world without war and without racism, a world that is more just and better to live in.

> So far your trips abroad have taken you mainly to the United States and Western Europe. You have never been to a Communist country; you have been only once to Africa – to Dakar – and once to Asia – to Kyoto; and in Latin America you travel mainly to attend meetings of bishops. Did you deliberately choose this 'Atlantic' orientation?

It's true that so far I have mainly visited industrialized countries. In a way it is more important and more urgent. If I can help the industrialized countries to see more clearly I shall be helping the whole of the Third World, not just Africa or Asia or Latin America. And in any case our minorities in the Third World manage better by themselves.

There are people not only in the poor countries but in the rich countries, even within the bourgeois structure, who hunger and thirst after justice, who want to see radical changes, but who are themselves victims of the system, prisoners. They must be helped and encouraged.

Very often when I go to North America or Europe employers or business executives say to me: 'But what can I do, Dom Helder? I should like my employees to work in better conditions, but what can I do?' I know that on their own they are helpless; if they paid higher wages, for instance, they would no longer be competitive and they'd be forced out of business.

The manager of an iron and steel works once invited me to

visit his factory. He told me I might examine his accounts, go anywhere I liked and talk to anyone I met. At lunchtime he was anxious to hear my impressions. But I changed the subject. So he insisted: 'Dom Helder, why don't you want to talk to me about the factory?' 'My friend, I think I have seen all the efforts that have been made here to prevent accidents, and pay good wages, and provide hygienic and healthy conditions, and facilities for further training. You even have a social club. All of it is admirable. But what about all the invisible signs?' 'Invisible signs?' 'Yes, everywhere I went in the factory I felt as though there were signs on the walls saying: "Worker! Anything, absolutely anything, will be granted to you on condition that you renounce the two bourgeois luxuries, intelligence and freedom!" ' He was an intelligent man, and he understood at once. 'You're right, Dom Helder. But what can I do? Even when I am here in charge of my factory I am only a poor human being. When I go to Belo Horizonte for the national meeting of all the directors in the group, I represent only a fraction: one eighteenth. And when I go to Luxembourg for the international meetings, I am nothing but a cog in the wheel.'

I understand quite well that it is difficult for key countries, as it is for key people, to deal with major problems. That is why I want to help them and encourage them.

> It was in order to help them that in 1971 you published a little book – the only book of yours which is not simply a collection of lectures – entitled *The Desert is Fertile*, with the sub-title: 'A guide for Abrahamic minorities'. In it you describe what you call your 'semi-failure', and above all your hope for the future.

My semi-failure was the illusions I had about the possibility of mobilizing institutions. My hope is the discovery of minorities. I didn't invent minorities: they are there, they exist, all you have to do is open your eyes and you can see them. Now we have to make people understand that the day will come – and it isn't far off – when all of these very different minorities will be united, without being unified.

And on that day . . . Forgive me for repeating myself, but there are some ideas that need repeating until they become convictions: on the day when we find a way of passing a current through all these minorities to unite them in common priority aims, we shall have discovered a force more powerful than nuclear power itself.

18

TOWARDS THE FINAL
DESTINATION

In the course of these interviews I have often asked
myself the question: is it you, Dom Helder, who have
changed your religion by stages, or is it religion that
has changed you? The Christianity you profess today
is quite different from the faith you professed, say,
when you were twenty . . .

How can I explain it? . . . The problem is that Christianity,
like truth, is so huge and rich that each of us can manage to
see only certain aspects of it. Christianity, like truth, does not
change: it is we who from time to time discover new aspects
of it. I remember when men flew around the moon for the
first time, and discovered the unknown, or unfamiliar, face
of our little neighbour. So it is not religion that has changed.
It is I who, by the grace of the Lord, and with the help of my
friends, my brothers, have had the opportunity of seeing
certain aspects of my religion that I did not see at first.
Christ is mysterious to us. In becoming a man He really
wanted to be one with us, but in the way that a father wants
to be one with his child, to understand him and be understood by him. But the child's ability to understand is
limited . . .

In re-living your life with you I get the impression
that each stage was for you merely a preparation for
the next. So where are your preparations leading?

What will your next stage be?

There comes a time when one has to find the courage, and even the happiness, to prepare to reach the final destination, to join the Father.

God does things in a very intelligent, very delicate way. Next to the blessing of a holy death, the greatest blessing is a kind old age. A kind old age means growing old on the outside without growing old inside. One by one, signs appear pointing to the final destination. You no longer have as much energy. You have difficulty in seeing, or hearing. As a matter of fact, all my faculties are still functioning: and I can still cope with my marathon trips abroad. But my heart tells me that the time has come to prepare to reach the final destination.

I think it is important to bear witness by really living one's death as the beginning of true life.

Of course I don't know how much longer the Lord is going to let me live.

I'm not preoccupied with death. My motto, the motto of my life and my episcopacy, is 'In manus tuas', 'In Thy Hands'. The Lord protects me so well that I can deliver myself with absolute trust into His fatherly hands. But I do still ask myself: 'How will my sister death come to me?' What I find most difficult to accept, but I do accept it, is the possibility that the Lord may choose to let me survive myself, I mean, to let my body survive my mind. When I first went to Rio de Janeiro people still talked about Cardinal Arcoverde, the first Brazilian and Latin American cardinal. He had been a great bishop, but at the end of his life he became a child again, you know . . . It isn't easy to accept the idea of surviving like that. But I do accept in advance even that form of death.

My friends often ask me why I am not more concerned about the threats against my life. Even the Holy Father asked me that question. But I replied: 'Holy Father, it is quite simple. I believe that sacrificing one's life for the sake of peace in the world and harmony between people is a blessing that no one deserves. So if the Lord offers me this blessing, without my doing anything to deserve it, there is absolutely no reason why I should worry about it!'

One of the greatest blessings of my life came to me recently during a vigil, when I realized the connection between the Last Supper and Calvary. On Maundy Thursday Christ was there with His disciples. He said mass, and it really was mass: He blessed the bread, He blessed the wine, He made an offering, He administered the sacrament. And then the mass continued mysteriously at Calvary. Every mass that has been said in the world, that is said now, and that will be said in the future is similarly continued at Calvary. That is what struck me . . . No one can stop at the Last Supper. Even Christ Himself, the only Son, one with His Father, felt abandoned: 'My God, my God, why hast Thou forsaken me?' It is a mysterious moment. So it is very important that we prepare ourselves for the Cross.

I continue with my work: but all the time I am quietly and calmly preparing to receive the death the Lord intends for me.

> You mentioned the blessing of a holy death. What is your idea of holiness?

Before I answer your question, I should like to explain something to you, quite simply.

Very often people – particularly poor people, humble people – imagine that you are better, more virtuous, than you really are, and want to canonize you, even while you are still alive. There is a story about Saint Francis of Assisi that I am very fond of, and that I find helpful. One day Francis and Brother Leo were out walking together. Suddenly Brother Leo called out: 'Brother Francis!' 'Yes, I am Brother Francis.' 'Be careful, Brother Francis! People are saying remarkable things about you! Be careful!' And Francis of Assisi replied: 'My friend, pray to the Lord that I may succeed in becoming what people think I am.' It is a beautiful reply.

There is a danger of losing your head when simple people begin to think of you as an extraordinary man, as a saint. But there are fortunately ways of guarding against it. For example, when I am about to go out and face a huge

audience which is applauding me and cheering me, I turn
to Christ and say to Him simply: 'Lord, this is Your triumphal entry into Jerusalem! I am just the little donkey
You are riding on!' And it's true.

Holiness . . . Well, 'Holy is the Lord'. Holiness is the Lord.
He is the only saint. There is only one Lord. But shared
holiness is not a privilege reserved for exceptional individuals. It is a duty for all of us. Through baptism we all
receive sanctifying grace, the grace that brings holiness. It is
very naive to think that being holy means seeing visions,
performing miracles, living a life that is very hard, very
extraordinary! Being holy means living with sanctifying
grace, living close to the Father, the Son and the Holy
Spirit, being one with your fellow human beings. And that
is a duty for all of us.

There is no single definition of holiness: there are dozens,
hundreds. But there is one that I am particularly fond of:
being holy means getting up immediately every time you
fall, with humility and joy. It doesn't mean never falling
into sin. It means being able to say: 'Yes, Lord, I have fallen
a thousand times. But thanks to You I have got up again a
thousand and one times.' That's all. I like thinking about
that.

When you are approaching death it is very tempting to
count your weaknesses and your failings and your sins, and
perhaps to lose courage. I think it is better not to count them
at all, not even to talk about them: 'Yes! My weaknesses and
my failings and my sins are innumerable, and very serious!
But there is something far greater than all my weaknesses and
failings and sins: the mercy of the Lord!'

Oh, I could tell you some wonderful things about the
mercy of the Lord! . . .

The ideal, really, would be to hear the Lord say to me on
the day of judgement: 'You will not be judged, because you
have refrained from judging others.' As you know Christ
said that we should be judged according to the standard we
had used for judging others. So if we refrain from judging,
we may even not be judged ourselves. Sometimes I try to
imagine Christ saying to me: 'Now look here, you've taken
this mercy business a bit too far: you've taken advantage of

it.' But that's impossible, because no one can go further than Christ in His mercy. He is mercy; He is understanding.

Oh, if only I could help – I can't do it, but the Lord can – to spread that understanding throughout the world. Understanding instead of judgement. Understanding doesn't always mean approval. But understanding instead of condemnation . . .

> Dom Helder, may I suggest a way of concluding these interviews? Would you like to express and summarize all that you have been saying in a 'Mass for the Century', like Teilhard de Chardin gave us in his 'Mass on the World'?

Yes, I should like to do that very much; and it would come easily to me because it is the kind of thing I often do. I love saying mass. When I am away from home it almost makes me sad – although I am afraid of sadness . . .

> You're afraid of sadness?

I am afraid of misguided sadness. There is often a trace of selfishness in sadness. Saint Francis called sadness 'the devil's sickness' . . .

It almost makes me sad when I can't say mass. But even if I can't physically say mass, you see – since it comes not from flesh and blood but from the Holy Spirit – I can still enact it. And there are some times when it is particularly appropriate. For example when I am flying. Suspended in an aeroplane at ten thousand or eleven thousand metres, we are more than ever in the hands of the Lord. 'The Spirit of the Lord was upon the waters . . .' He is upon the earth, among humanity. Communion, the offertory, the consecration: it's so easy at times like that. And you don't think only of the earth, which is so tiny, albeit so important since the Incarnation. You think really in terms of the universe. Often I launch myself into space, and sail away altogether . . . Simply to glorify the Lord . . .

19

MASS FOR THE CENTURY

O Century, our vehicle through time! This mass is being celebrated expressly for you.

But first of all let us have the courage to ask ourselves the question: what is a century worth by God's standards? What is a century worth in relation to the progress of humanity?

By God's standards – forgive us, Century – a hundred years is no more than a drop in the ocean. When scholars investigate the age of the universe they lose themselves in millions and millions of years. It is frightening even to think in terms of light-years.

In relation to the progress of humanity, with the wild acceleration of history, ten years in modern times are the equivalent of fifty in the past, and twenty years almost call for centenary celebrations.

I shall not forget, O Century my friend, that I was almost present at your birth; and with a little effort I shall accompany you to the start of the next millennium ...

But in any case I am one with Christ, one with Him, as I begin this Eucharist, this thanksgiving in your name ...

Do you know what I thank the Creator and Father for most of all? I thank Him for uniting me, in Christ, with all human beings of every race, every colour and creed ...

Christ teaches us more and more that all of us, absolutely all of us, without exception, have the same father; and that, consequently, we are all brothers! And further, we human beings sense that our fraternity extends to include all creatures, animated or inert, great or small. All of us emerged from the hands of the Creator!

Lending our voices joyfully to the stones and the seas, to the winds and the stars, to the trees and the animals, we are aware that above all we are brothers to our fellow men, sharing adventures and dangers, misery and glory . . .

O Century, our vehicle through time! Is it an exaggeration to say that today more than ever man is participating in the creative power of the Father in mastering nature and completing the work of creation? Kindling fire and inventing the wheel were among the first results of this participation. But today electronic computers are multiplying at an astonishing rate, and discoveries like nuclear energy and the boldness of journeys into space almost seem like an unwarranted invasion of God's own territory. But no! Our Father is incapable of jealousy! The more we advance, the more we attempt, the more we glorify the Creator and Father!

But it is a pity, O Century our friend, that while we are capable of both banishing misery from the earth and destroying all life in the universe, we continue to play this stupid game of manufacturing armaments which we know are powerful enough to mean suicide for all mankind.

It is a pity, O Century our friend, that as we begin to reach out towards the stars we leave behind us on earth an absurdity, a folly, an aberration: more than two-thirds of humanity living in sub-human conditions, suffering from poverty and starvation . . .

But what a joy it is, O Century, to see that God really isn't selfish. How the Creator and Father rejoices to make man His co-creator, how the Son of God, the Redeemer of man and the universe, rejoices to make us His co-liberators!

Christ, the Son of God made man, who made Himself our brother, urges us today more than ever to liberate ourselves and liberate our brothers and sisters from sin and the consequences of sin, from selfishness and the consequences of selfishness.

It is a pity, O Century, that as we continue to extend the limits of our intelligence and creativity we continue to be so limited, so grossly selfish and so incapable of imagining a world without empires to control and subjugate it. Incapable of imagining a world without oppressors and oppressed ...

Nevertheless, O Century, in every country, and every race, and every religion, in every human group, the Spirit of God continues to inspire minorities who are resolved to make any sacrifice in order to create a world that is better to live in, more just and more humane: in order to liberate the world from the increasingly heavy and stifling structures that oppress practically all men.

What a joy it is to know that, without recourse to armed violence, young people – who have most reason for living! – will discover the secret of union between regions, between countries, between continents, between worlds. And then, animated by a Love that is more powerful than death, we shall conquer war! We shall abolish racism! We shall suppress empires!

In centuries to come, human weakness will devise other oppressive structures. Selfishness will re-establish its ascendancy. Among the oppressed, underdogs, down-trodden, you will find many divisions, suspicions, cracks and conflicts.

But rejoice, O Century our friend: we shall do the possible and the impossible to ensure that you pass on to the twenty-first century the victorious flame of a world without oppressors or oppressed, a world of brothers!

Onward, Century! Don't be an outsider at our Eucharist. Take an active part in our thanksgiving. Without hypocrisy, without pretending to be the greatest or the best, resolve to make any sacrifice in order to reach the threshold of the year two thousand deserving the title 'the century of liberation'!

Do you know what I am asking of you now? That you awaken hopes, that you mobilize youth, and that you fight for the cause of unity.

You will find many people's hopes are faded, intermittent or languishing. Many people are sceptical – or in despair ...

To those who are fortunate enough to believe in God the Creator and Father, you will point out that God did not create the world in order to amuse Himself at our expense. He created the world and man out of love. Hatred will not have the last word.

To those who don't believe in God but have faith in man, you will point out that there is no point in half a faith. The only effective faith is total faith. True faith radiates hope and love.

If you meet young people of sixteen or eighteen or twenty who claim that life is absurd and question you about the meaning of their lives, make them understand that losing the joy of living is a sign of precocious old age. Make everyone understand, men and women of all ages, that we have a thousand reasons for living. They are wrong to think they have arrived too late in a world that is too old, where everything is already settled and there is nothing more to do!

Among the oppressed you will find a profusion of divisions, splits, distrust and conflict . . . Oppressors are skilful at sowing discord among the oppressed. It was no coincidence that at the supreme moment of His life Christ asked His Father for unity among His people.

Suggest, teach, persuade: the day will come when all the world's minorities will unite to construct a world that is more just and more humane, the day when we shall finally discover the nuclear force of Love!